By Water and the Spirit

Making Connections for Identity and Ministry

GAYLE CARLTON FELTON

This study guide includes the full text of *By Water and the Spirit:
A United Methodist Understanding of Baptism,* adopted by the
1996 General Conference of The United Methodist Church.

DISCIPLESHIP RESOURCES

P.O. BOX 340003 • NASHVILLE, TN 37203-0003
www.discipleshipresources.org

Revised and reprinted 1998, 1999, 2002, 2006, 2007, 2010.

Book and cover design by Sharon Anderson

Images ©1997 PhotoDisc, Inc.

Library of Congress Card Catalog No. 96-86603

ISBN 978-0-88177-201-2

DR201

Contents

Introduction

United Methodists have many questions about the sacrament of baptism. The purpose of *By Water and the Spirit* is to attempt to answer those questions. It is significant in the life of the church because it tries to clear up some of the confusion that sometimes prevents us from appreciating this wonderful gift that God has given us. *By Water and the Spirit* is an official statement by our church to be used in teaching our people how United Methodists understand and practice baptism. It is a resource for pastors, teachers, small group leaders, curriculum writers, families, and others. It is intended to be a tool for making Christians, for fashioning people into disciples of Christ, and equipping them for ministry.

This study edition of *By Water and the Spirit* is specifically designed to be a document for practical use rather than a presentation of abstract theology. Its goal is to help United Methodists live more faithfully as God's baptized people. The resource is organized into six teaching and learning sessions. In some sessions, there may be more material than you can cover, and participants can be encouraged to continue their study beyond the group. (Every participant should have a copy of this study book.) Each session contains three types of material: the text of the document approved by the General Conference, commentary about that text, and suggestions for teaching it. Quotations from *The Book of Discipline* within the reprinted text of *By Water and the Spirit: A United Methodist Understanding of Baptism* reflect the wording of the 1992 edition, the version in effect at the time the document was approved by General Conference. Quotations from *The Book of Discipline* within the study commentary use the wording of the 2004 edition.

Please remember that the document itself is the primary resource, and you should focus on it. Other material is intended to offer further help. It is my hope that you will be enriched by this study and motivated to explore other aspects of our United Methodist history, theology, and practice.

Gayle Carlton Felton

By Water and the Spirit: A United Methodist Understanding of Baptism

Contemporary United Methodism is attempting to recover and revitalize its understanding of baptism. To do this, we must look to our heritage as Methodists and Evangelical United Brethren and, indeed, to the foundations of Christian Tradition. Throughout our history, baptism has been viewed in diverse and even contradictory ways. An enriched understanding of baptism, restoring the Wesleyan blend of sacramental and evangelical aspects, will enable United Methodists to participate in the sacrament with renewed appreciation for this gift of God's grace.

Within the Methodist tradition, baptism has long been a subject of much concern, even controversy. John Wesley retained the sacramental theology which he received from his Anglican heritage. He taught that in baptism a child was cleansed of the guilt of original sin, initiated into the covenant with God, admitted into the Church, made an heir of the divine kingdom, and spiritually born anew. While baptism was neither essential to nor sufficient for salvation, it was the "ordinary means" that God had designated for

WHAT DO WE BELIEVE?

I once read an account of an imaginary softball tournament being played between churches of various denominations—Baptists, Lutherans, Presbyterians, Roman Catholics, and others—including United Methodists. At one point in the game, a member of another denominational team exclaimed, "Oh, we just love to play ball with the United Methodists! They don't care what the rules are!" This little story is amusing, but it is also somewhat disturbing. Is it really true that we do not care about any standards? Are we a church that allows people to believe in anything and to do whatever they wish? Should we be such a church?

Most of us would probably agree that we do not have to think and act alike about everything. Indeed, faithful United Methodist Christians can and do disagree about many areas of our beliefs and practices. God does not deal with all of us in the same way. Our varying experiences—including families and friends, education and work, geographic regions and political loyalties—affect our ideas. We need to allow other Christians to disagree with us on some matters without doubting their commitment to Christ. God uses other people, especially those who think differently, to help us learn more about how to be faithful disciples.

Just because we may disagree about some things does not imply that "anything goes" or that we "don't care what the rules are." There are certain basic beliefs that make up the foundation of Christianity—for example, that God revealed the divine nature and purpose to us in Jesus Christ. There are certain ethical standards by which Christians are to live—for example, that we act lovingly toward other people. Certain other beliefs are characteristic of the particular denominations into which the church of Jesus Christ is divided. Examples of this include: the Baptist mode of baptism by immersion; the Disciples of Christ practice of weekly Communion; the Pentecostal emphasis upon the gifts of the Holy Spirit; the Society of Friends' custom of worshiping in silence; and the Roman Catholic requirement that only males can be priests. I tend to think that no denomination has a monopoly on all of God's truth, and we should respect and learn from each other.

applying the benefits of the work of Christ in human lives.

On the other hand, although he affirmed the regenerating grace of infant baptism, he also insisted upon the necessity of adult conversion for those who have fallen from grace. A person who matures into moral accountability must respond to God's grace in repentance and faith. Without personal decision and commitment to Christ, the baptismal gift is rendered ineffective.

Baptism for Wesley, therefore, was a part of the lifelong process of salvation. He saw spiritual rebirth as a twofold experience in the normal process of Christian development—to be received through baptism in infancy and through commitment to Christ later in life. Salvation included both God's initiating activity of grace and a willing human response.

In its development in the United States, Methodism was unable to maintain this Wesleyan balance of sacramental and evangelical emphases. Access to the sacraments was limited during the late eighteenth and early nineteenth centuries when the Methodist movement was largely under the leadership of laypersons who were not authorized to administer them. On the American frontier where human ability and action were stressed, the revivalistic call for individual decision-making, though important, was subject to exaggeration. The sacramental teachings of Wesley tended to be ignored. In this setting, while infant baptism continued not only to be practiced, but also to be vigorously defended, its significance became weakened and ambiguous.

United Methodists share many beliefs and morals with other Christian denominations. But we also have certain points that have been strongly emphasized throughout our history. These are our distinctive and defining positions. Some examples include our insistence that God's grace is freely available to all who will accept it, that we are to grow in holiness throughout our lives, and that one's saving relationship with Christ can be lost by sin.

THE SACRAMENT OF BAPTISM

It is through the sacrament of baptism that we are given our identity as people for whom Jesus Christ lived, died, and was resurrected. In baptism we are initiated into the Christian church; we are incorporated into the community of God's people, the body of Christ. By baptism we are commissioned into ministry; we are called to continue the work of Christ for the redemption of the world. As we realize who we are (by God's grace), what kind of community we comprise, and with what mission we have been charged, we eagerly seek the instruments that can aid us. *By Water and the Spirit* is offered as an instrument for nurturing our faith. It is a teaching tool, planned with the aim of deepening commitment and providing fuller knowledge and experience of the ongoing process of salvation. It is an instrument for evangelistic outreach, for communicating to other people the good news of Jesus Christ. It is an instrument for social justice efforts, for challenging and changing the forces of oppression and violence. It is an instrument for proclaiming and portraying the radical nature of baptism and its consequences in our lives.

To study baptism is to study the Christian gospel. Almost every aspect of our faith can be viewed through the focusing lens of baptism. The sacrament teaches us much about who God is and how God acts toward us. It reveals to us who we are as human beings—our sad, sinful condition and the triumphant purpose that God has for our lives. How can our brokenness be healed? How can we, both as individuals and a society, become the people God created us to be? How are we to be made reconciled, meaningful, joyous, compassionate, just? What does the church have to do with all of this? What is so special about the church, compared to other human institutions? How does God's love come to us through the church? What does it mean to speak of the sacraments as special means of grace?

OUR ROOTS

As we begin our study of baptism, it will be helpful to sketch the history of the Christian understanding of the sacraments. Both baptism and Holy Communion have been practiced by Christians since the time of Christ. Before the Protestant

Later toward the end of the nineteenth century, the theological views of much of Methodism were influenced by a new set of ideas which had become dominant in American culture. These ideas included optimism about the progressive improvement of humankind and confidence in the social benefits of scientific discovery, technology, and education. Assumptions of original sin gave way before the assertion that human nature was essentially unspoiled. In this intellectual milieu, the old evangelical insistence upon conversion and spiritual rebirth seemed quaint and unnecessary.

Thus the creative Wesleyan synthesis of sacramentalism and evangelicalism was torn asunder and both its elements devalued. As a result, infant baptism was variously interpreted and often reduced to a ceremony of dedication. Adult baptism was sometimes interpreted as a profession of faith and public acknowledgment of God's grace, but was more often viewed simply as an act of joining the Church. By the middle of the twentieth century, Methodism in general had ceased to understand baptism as authentically sacramental. Rather than an act of divine grace, it was seen as an expression of human choice.

Baptism was also a subject of concern and controversy in the Evangelical and United Brethren traditions that were brought together in 1946 in The Evangelical United Brethren Church. Their early pietistic revivalism, based upon belief in the availability of divine grace and the freedom of human choice, emphasized bringing people to salvation through Christian experience. In the late nineteenth and early

Reformation in the sixteenth century, the two major parts of the Christian church were Roman Catholicism and Eastern Orthodoxy. In both of these churches certain ceremonies (including confirmation, penance, marriage, ordination, and extreme unction) were observed as sacraments—rites through which God's grace comes to God's people. When Martin Luther in Germany and John Calvin in Switzerland broke away from the Roman Catholic Church, they kept only baptism and Holy Communion as sacraments. Other Protestant reformers led groups that interpreted these rites differently. Some, such as Ulrich Zwingli in Switzerland, practiced baptism and Holy Communion as occasions for remembering Christ and our profession of faith, rather than as means of grace. The radical reformers, or Anabaptists, taught that baptism is an individual's profession of faith; therefore, only believing adults should be baptized. The family tree of United Methodism can be traced through the Roman Catholic-Lutheran-Calvinist branch, particularly as it developed in the Church of England. As a German Reformed minister, Philip William Otterbein, chief founder of the United Brethren in Christ, was grounded in the Lutheran tradition. The Evangelical Church was begun by the work of Jacob Albright whose background was Lutheran and whose shaping influence was Methodist. Clearly, United Methodism has major roots in the sacramental tradition of Christianity.

Along with its roots in the sacramental tradition, United Methodism is also deeply grounded in Christianity's evangelical tradition. All of the founders of the various groups that came together as The United Methodist Church were deeply influenced by pietism and its emphasis upon personal religious experience, conversion, and commitment to Christ. The blending of various influences to produce United Methodism can be illustrated by remembering that another founder of the United Brethren was Martin Boehm, a Mennonite in the Anabaptist tradition. This combination of elements to form a vital and life-transforming faith is characteristic of the work and thought of John Wesley.

While we usually think of John Wesley as a Methodist, it is important to remember that he lived and died as an Anglican priest. Much of his theology comes out of the teachings of the Church of England. (For us, as present-day United Methodists, this means that our closest "relative" is the Episcopal Church.) While questions about baptism were not extremely controversial in Wesley's day, he, nevertheless, preached and wrote a good deal on the subject, usually referring to the baptism of infants. He taught that baptism is a good gift from God to the church, a significant part of God's plan for bringing people to salvation. Christian parents are expected to bring their infant

twentieth centuries, both Evangelical and United Brethren theologians stressed the importance of baptism as integral to the proclamation of the gospel, as a rite initiating persons into the covenant community (paralleling circumcision), and as a sign of the new birth, that gracious divine act by which persons are redeemed from sin and reconciled to God. The former Evangelical Church consistently favored the baptism of infants. The United Brethren provided for the baptism of both infants and adults. Following the union of 1946, The Evangelical United Brethren Church adopted a ritual that included services of baptism for infants and adults, and also a newly created service for the dedication of infants that had little precedent in official rituals of either of the former churches.

The 1960-64 revision of *The Methodist Hymnal*, including rituals, gave denominational leaders an opportunity to begin to recover the sacramental nature of baptism in contemporary Methodism. The General Commission on Worship sounded this note quite explicitly in its introduction to the new ritual in 1964:

In revising the Order for the Administration of Baptism, the Commission on Worship has endeavored to keep in mind that baptism is a sacrament, and to restore it to the Evangelical-Methodist concept set forth in our Articles of Religion....Due recognition was taken of the critical reexamination of the theology of the Sacrament of Baptism which is currently taking place in ecumenical circles, and of its theological content and implications.

children to receive God's grace through baptism. Despite Wesley's understanding of the importance of the sacrament, he knew that God could bring people to salvation without their having received it. He insisted strongly that simply having been baptized is no guarantee of anyone's salvation. Baptism is a part of the lifelong process by which God works in our lives. The grace that comes to us in baptism must be responded to and accepted in repentance and faith as we mature. One of Wesley's most outstanding contributions to Christian theology was this creative synthesis of "sacramentalism" and "evangelicalism." He blended and balanced the free gift of divine grace, which is made available to us through various means (including the sacraments), with the necessity of our human response of faith and holy living.

When Methodism came to America with the European immigrants in the 1760s, it entered a world very different from its birthplace in Great Britain. Wesley always insisted that only properly ordained people be allowed to baptize and serve the Lord's Supper. The Revolutionary War for independence from Great Britain made it impossible for American Methodists to continue receiving the sacraments in Anglican churches as Wesley had envisioned. Until the official creation of The Methodist Episcopal Church at the Christmas Conference of 1784, there were no ordained Methodist ministers to offer the sacraments. Indeed, one of the pressing reasons for setting up a separate church was to be able to ordain ministers to meet the demands for baptism and Holy Communion. The sacraments certainly continued to be practiced in American Methodism. There were services for both sacraments even at the camp meetings of the nineteenth century. However, it is undeniably true that Wesley's creative synthesis—blending and balancing sacramentalism and evangelicalism—weakened and fell apart in the American environment. Worship services tended to be informal occasions made up of preaching, singing, Bible reading, and praying. The evangelical side of Methodism, with its stress upon the individual experience of salvation, became dominant.

Unfortunately, this evangelical aspect of Methodism also declined in the latter years of the nineteenth century and early decades of the twentieth. The emphases on sin, repentance, faith, conversion, rebirth, and holiness became increasingly unpopular. These changes occurred, in varying degrees, in all of the predecessor denominations that have now merged to constitute United Methodism—The Methodist Episcopal Church; The Methodist Episcopal Church, South; The Methodist Protestant Church; The Church of the United Brethren in Christ; and The Evangelical Church.

The commission provided a brief historical perspective demonstrating that the understanding of baptism as a sacrament had been weakened, if not discarded altogether, over the years. Many in the Church regarded baptism, both of infants and adults, as a dedication rather than as a sacrament. The commission pointed out that in a dedication we make a gift of a life to God for God to accept, while in a sacrament God offers the gift of God's unfailing grace for us to accept. The 1964 revision of the ritual of the sacrament of baptism began to restore the rite to its original and historic meaning as a sacrament.

In the 1989 *The United Methodist Hymnal*, the Services of the Baptismal Covenant I, II and IV (taken from the 1984 official ritual of the denomination as printed in *The Book of Services*) continue this effort to reemphasize the historic significance of baptism. These rituals, in accenting the reality of sin and of regeneration, the initiating of divine grace and the necessity of repentance and faith, are consistent with the Wesleyan combination of sacramentalism and evangelicalism.

United Methodism is not alone in the need to recover the significance of baptism nor in its work to do so. Other Christian communions are also reclaiming the importance of this sacrament for Christian faith and life. To reach the core of the meaning and practice of baptism, all have found themselves led back through the life of the Church to the Apostolic Age. An ecumenical convergence has emerged from this effort, as can be seen in the widely acclaimed document, *Baptism, Eucharist, and Ministry* (1982).

The understanding of baptism was significantly affected and altered. There was lessened appreciation for the church and its sacraments as means of divine grace, as well as a reduced sense of sin and need for spiritual transformation. I contend that many of the present-day difficulties of United Methodism—as shown starkly by our alarming membership decline for the last four decades—have their roots in this tearing apart and discarding of our theological heritage.

IN RECENT YEARS

By the middle of the twentieth century, infant baptism was commonly understood by the various denominations of our tradition as simply an act of dedication in which parents thanked God for the child and pledged themselves to raise him or her in the Christian faith. Little consideration was given to the role of God or to the church as a community of faith. Baptized children were officially designated as "preparatory members" of the church, but were usually treated as outsiders until they participated in services called "reception into membership," or later called "confirmation." Such services were often viewed as "joining the church." In many cases baptized children were not welcomed to take Holy Communion until they had been through such a service and made their vows publicly. These practices clearly reveal that infant baptism was rarely understood as a means of grace through which God is truly acting. The frequent use of the term "christening" is convincing evidence that infant baptism was seldom considered to be "the real thing." In teaching many diverse groups about baptism, I have heard no question repeated more often than that of christening. Many United Methodists are astonished to learn that none of our churches has ever had an official service of christening separate from infant baptism. No, not even if they were told so by the preacher!

By the 1960s many leaders of the church were realizing and becoming concerned that we had lost our appreciation for baptism as a sacrament. In the baptismal ritual of the 1964 *Hymnal*, there is an effort to begin the process of recovery.

The new rituals for baptismal services in the current *Hymnal* substantially show more movement in the direction of reclaiming the sacramental aspects of our heritage. Plainly, United Methodism is seeking to return to the Wesleyan synthesis that had been largely lost. In this effort to recover the significance of baptism as an act of God's grace in the church, we are joined by other denominations doing the same thing.

When the 1988 General Conference approved the current "Services of the Baptismal Covenant," it recognized the need for the church to study the meaning of baptism more

Established by the General Conference of 1988 and authorized to continue its work by the General Conference of 1992, the Committee to Study Baptism is participating in this process by offering a theological and functional understanding of baptism as embodied in the ritual of The United Methodist Church. In so doing, the broad spectrum of resources of Scripture, Christian tradition, and the Methodist-Evangelical United Brethren experience has been taken into account. The growing ecumenical consensus has assisted us in our thinking.

comprehensively. The General Conference authorized the General Board of Discipleship to form a committee that would focus on this task. At the 1992 General Conference, the document produced by this committee was recommended for study throughout the denomination. Cokesbury published the document, accompanied by a study guide and a questionnaire for feedback by individuals and groups. Taking these responses into consideration, the committee rewrote the document. In its revised form, *By Water and the Spirit: A United Methodist Understanding of Baptism*, was approved as an official interpretive statement on baptism for the church by the 1996 General Conference. The study edition that you are now reading is designed to encourage the use and assist in the understanding of this statement.

Leader Helps

RESOURCES AND MATERIALS

- Each participant will need a copy of this study guide. Encourage the participants to make notes in their guides.
- Copies of *The United Methodist Hymnal*

SESSION GUIDE

1. Begin by inviting the students to discuss the following questions:
   - Is it true that United Methodists do not care about standards?
   - Are we a church in which people can believe and do whatever they wish?
   - Should we be such a church?

   (If the class is large, divide it into smaller groups.)

2. Lead the group in listing some of the things about which contemporary Christians disagree and in considering the reasons for such disagreements. The point here is not to persuade, but to make it clear that all Christians do not believe and live exactly alike.

3. Using the information in the section "The Sacrament of Baptism" on page 2, review the goals of the study, reminding the participants that baptism is not an isolated subject, but one to which every aspect of the Christian faith can be related. If the participants have not had the opportunity to read the first chapter of the study guide, allow them time to read it.

4. Use the information in the section "Our Roots" (p. 2) and the chart on page 51 to summarize our historical understandings and practices of baptism. Take time to trace the formation of The United Methodist Church through the reunion of three major Methodist branches in 1939 to form The Methodist Church and its merger in 1968 with the Evangelical United Brethren Church. Use the chart on page 52 to help with this.

5. Have the participants read the section "In Recent Years" (p. 5). Invite participants to describe their own current understandings of both infant and adult baptism and to reflect upon how their ideas have been influenced by the developments expressed in the section they have just read. Be careful to avoid making people feel criticized.

6. Discuss the difference between a dedication and a sacrament. Emphasize "that in a dedication we make a gift of a life to God for God to accept, while in a sacrament God offers the gift of God's unfailing grace for us to accept." Ask participants to share their memories about the use of the term "christening."

7. Distribute copies of *The United Methodist Hymnal* to all participants. Have them find the "Services of the Baptismal Covenant," noting that the location of these rituals toward the front is, in itself, symbolic of the renewed appreciation of their significance. Allow time for a very brief look at the various services, and state that upcoming study sessions will focus much more closely upon them.

8. Close the session with an opportunity for questions and comments. Ask the participants to read Session Two in preparation for the next session.

TO EXPAND THIS STUDY

- Use some of the excellent resources that are available to teach what it means to be a United Methodist Christian. A classic that has been repeatedly revised since 1955 is *Major United Methodist Beliefs* by Mack B. Stokes. Newer materials are *Living Our Beliefs: The United Methodist Way* by Kenneth Carder; *Why I Am a United Methodist* by William H. Willimon; *Meet the Methodists: An Introduction to The United Methodist Church* by Charles L. Allen; *The United Methodist Primer* by Chester Custer; and *The Making of Methodism* by Barrie Tabraham. Curriculum resources in the area include *This We Believe*, *We Are United Methodists*, and *Faithful Members*. All of these are available from Cokesbury. For purposes of this study on baptism, these resources can provide excellent background information. Familiarity with them may encourage participants to undertake further study—both in groups and as individuals.

- Many United Methodists would enjoy and benefit from knowing more about John Wesley, our founder. Several excellent videos are available and may be obtained through your annual conference media center. Suggestions include: *John Wesley, Proud Methodist* and *Through Wesley's England*.

- For more information about Wesley's understanding and practice of baptism, see the first two chapters of *This Gift of Water: The Practice and Theology of Baptism Among Methodists in America* by Gayle Felton.

- Read and discuss the following quotation by Wayne Clymer:

  > The theology of baptism is underdeveloped in the Methodist tradition. We believe that we should baptize, but we expect little from it. People bring their children to be baptized much as they bring them to the doctor to be vaccinated. They have it done and hope that it will do some good. The congregation serves as spectator. Parents take vows which very often they have heard for the first time and, under the pressure of the situation, may not hear at all (*Membership Means Discipleship*, pp. 25-26).

- Use these quotations from Wesley to stimulate discussion.

  > In the ordinary way, there is no other means of entering into the Church or into heaven...the benefit of this [the atoning death of Christ] is to be received through the means which he hath appointed; through baptism in particular, which is the ordinary means he hath appointed for that purpose; and to which God hath tied us, though he may not have tied himself (From "Treatise on Baptism," 10:192).

  > Lean no more on the staff of that broken reed, that ye *were* born again in baptism. Who denies that ye were then made children of God, and heirs of the kingdom of heaven? But, notwithstanding this, ye are now children of the devil. Therefore ye must be born again (From "The Marks of the New Birth," 5:222).

  > [In baptism] a principle of grace is infused, which will not be wholly taken away, unless we quench the Holy Spirit of God by long-continued wickedness....Baptism doth now save us, if we live answerable thereto; if we repent, believe, and obey the gospel...(From "Treatise on Baptism," 10:192).

Who Are We?
Who Does God Intend Us To Be?

We Are Saved by God's Grace

The Human Condition

As told in the first chapters of Genesis, in creation God made human beings in the image of God—a relationship of intimacy, dependence, and trust. We are open to the indwelling presence of God and given freedom to work with God to accomplish the divine will and purpose for all of creation and history. To be human as God intended is to have loving fellowship with God and to reflect the divine nature in our lives as fully as possible.

Tragically, as Genesis 3 recounts, we are unfaithful to that relationship. The result is a thorough distortion of the image of God in us and the degrading of the whole of creation. Through prideful overreach or denial of our God-given responsibilities, we exalt our own will, invent our own values, and rebel against God. Our very being is dominated by an inherent inclination toward evil which has traditionally been called original sin. It is a universal human condition and affects all aspects of life. Because of our condition of sin, we are separated from God, alienated from one another, hostile to the natural world, and even at odds with our own best selves. Sin may be expressed as errant priorities, as deliberate wrongdoing,

A Sinful People

Writing in the late 1930s, theologian H. Richard Niebuhr criticized a kind of weak, superficial Christianity that taught, "A God without wrath brought [people] without sin into a kingdom without judgment through the ministrations of a Christ without a cross" (*The Kingdom of God in America*, p. 193). This kind of cheap and falsely optimistic Christianity remains a dangerous heresy today.

At the very heart of the Christian faith is the realization that we are broken and needy people who are saved by the gracious act of God in Jesus Christ. The traditions that make up United Methodism have always insisted that saving grace is freely available to all who will receive it.

The idea of sin is rather "out of style" in our contemporary society. We prefer to talk about "dysfunction," "maladjustment," "relationship difficulties," or "social problems." Unfortunately, this unwillingness to look honestly at sin is not limited to the secular society; it also deeply afflicts the church. One of the most common criticisms of our current baptismal liturgies is aimed at the "Renunciation of Sin" section (see p. 34 in *The United Methodist Hymnal*). Some pastors even go so far as to edit the ritual by omitting the references to "the spiritual forces of wickedness," "the evil powers of this world," and "your sin." This practice is even more frequent when the service is that of the baptism of an infant. Frankly, I find this reluctance to speak of sin to be quite puzzling. How can anyone so much as glance at the daily newspaper headlines or casually listen to the radio and television newscasts without being confronted with the powerful, inescapable reality of sin? How can anyone, especially people who understand themselves to be Christians, view their own image in a mirror or pause for a fleeting moment of reflection, and not be faced with the continual struggle against sin? I am convinced that much of the weakness of present-day Christianity results from our unwillingness to acknowledge the presence and effects of sin. After all, if there is no sin, there is no need for a Savior. If we are not lost, we do not need the Good Shepherd to find us, much less die for us! Unless we accept the reality of sin, the Christian gospel simply does not make sense.

as apathy in the face of need, as cooperation with oppression and injustice. Evil is cosmic as well as personal; it afflicts both individuals and the institutions of our human society. The nature of sin is represented in Baptismal Covenants I, II and IV in *The United Methodist Hymnal* by the phrases "the spiritual forces of wickedness" and "the evil powers of this world," as well as "your sin." Before God all persons are lost, helpless to save themselves, and in need of divine mercy and forgiveness.

The Divine Initiative of Grace

While we have turned from God, God has not abandoned us. Instead, God graciously and continuously seeks to restore us to that loving relationship for which we were created, to make us into the persons that God would have us be. To this end God acts preveniently, that is, before we are aware of it, reaching out to save humankind. The Old Testament records the story of God's acts in the history of the covenant community of Israel to work out the divine will and purpose. In the New Testament story, we learn that God came into this sinful world in the person of Jesus Christ to reveal all that the human mind can comprehend about who God is and who God would have us be. Through Christ's death and resurrection, the power of sin and death was overcome and we are set free to again be God's own people (1 Peter 2:9). Since God is the only initiator and source of grace, all grace is prevenient in that it precedes and enables any movement that we can make toward God. Grace brings us

A BIBLICAL GUIDE

The opening chapters of the Bible (Genesis 1-3) can guide our understanding here. It is not necessary to view these stories as historical or scientific treatises. What is essential is what they teach us about who we are, and who God intends us to be. The Creation accounts affirm that sin is not the first reality. These stories portray the action of a powerful God who brought all of creation into existence and who then pronounced it "good." God crowns the created universe with human beings, male and female, who are loved by God and who are intended to live in a loving relationship with God, with each other, and with the natural world. Tragically, human beings reject God's purpose for them; they put their own desires in place of the divine will; they try to live apart from God. These actions of human unfaithfulness result in separation from God, in alienation from each other, in antagonism to the natural environment. Sin is not simply the human actions of disobedience; it is more profoundly the very condition of human life. We are in a state of sin; we are sinful creatures who live in a world that we have made sinful. Sin distorts our vision of God and of ourselves. Sin is much more than individual actions; it corrupts the institutions and practices of our whole society. The stories of Genesis 1-3 are not just tales of long ago about a man named Adam and a woman named Eve in a garden called Eden. These stories are accounts of the lives of each of us, here and now. Every day the serpent speaks and we respond. This is the bad news—we have made a mess of our lives, such a big mess that we are not able to clean it up by ourselves.

GOD'S SAVING GRACE

We have heard the bad news of sin. Now we listen for the *good news*—the gospel—the story of God's action to save us.

God is not willing to leave us in sin; God acts to save us. The entire story of the Bible is the story of God's efforts to bring us back into the loving relationships for which we are created. The God of the Bible is a God who acts in and through the events of human history. In the Old Testament, we see that God chose a particular people—the Hebrews, Israelites, or children of Israel, later known as the Jews—to be an instrument of divine purpose. Through the life of the Hebrew community, God sought to make plain how God's people were to live. By revealing the divine law and raising up political leaders, priests, and prophets, God strove to rescue human beings from the consequences of sin and to restore their relationship with God. The New Testament is the record of God's greatest action to make our salvation possible. God takes human form in the person of Jesus the Christ and reveals to us as much of the divine nature and

to an awareness of our sinful predicament and of our inability to save ourselves; grace motivates us to repentance and gives us the capacity to respond to divine love. In the words of the baptismal ritual: "All this is God's gift, offered to us without price" (*The United Methodist Hymnal*, page 33).

The Necessity of Faith for Salvation

Faith is both a gift of God and a human response to God. It is the ability and willingness to say "yes" to the divine offer of salvation. Faith is our awareness of our utter dependence upon God, the surrender of our selfish wills, the trusting reliance upon divine mercy. The candidate for baptism answers "I do" to the question "Do you confess Jesus Christ as your Savior, put your whole trust in his grace, and promise to serve him as your Lord...?" (*The United Methodist Hymnal*, p. 34). Our personal response of faith requires conversion in which we turn away from sin and turn instead to God. It entails a decision to commit our lives to the Lordship of Christ, an acceptance of the forgiveness of our sins, the death of our old selves, an entering into a new life of the Spirit—being born again (John 3:3-5, 2 Corinthians 5:17). All persons do not experience this spiritual rebirth in the same way. For some, there is a singular, radical moment of conversion. For others, conversion may be the dawning and growing realization that one has been constantly loved by God and has a personal reliance upon Christ. John Wesley described his own experience by saying, "I felt

will as our human minds are capable of comprehending. Finally, Christ suffers death, bearing the burden of human sinfulness and is restored to life, revealing the power of God. Christ's ministry, death, and resurrection guarantee God's ultimate victory over sin and evil, and make it possible for each of us to share in that victory. God continues the work of Christ in the world through the Christian church and the lives of individual Christians. We are to be engaged in the great task of showing the world the saving love of God and achieving reconciliation. Toward the end of the Bible, we find the vision of the created order restored to the loving relationship with God for which it was originally designed before the intrusion of sin. We are assured that, even in the face of sin, suffering, and injustice, God and God's people are at work and that the divine purpose will be fulfilled at last.

John Wesley spoke and wrote much about what he called prevenient grace—the grace that "comes before." This means that God must act first to enable us to act. Because our lives are so marred by sin, we are unable to achieve our own salvation. But God gives each person the capacity to respond to the offer of saving grace. We are people of moral responsibility because, through prevenient grace, we have "response-ability." As we respond in trusting faith, God gives more grace for our empowerment to grow in holiness of life. As the early Methodists affirmed repeatedly: "Grace is free in all, free for all."

REPENTANCE

As Wesley's description of his Aldersgate experience illustrates, to have faith is to trust—to trust God instead of ourselves, to trust God as we know God in Jesus Christ instead of any person, power, or possession. Faith requires our realization of the reality of sin in our lives and our helplessness to free ourselves from it. When we become aware of the sin that separates us from God and from others, we grieve and desire change. This is repentance—sorrow for sin and turning our lives around. Repentance is doing an "about-face"; it is ceasing to go in one direction and turning to go in another. In the baptismal services of the early church, repentance was symbolically expressed by the person facing one direction to renounce sin and then turning to face the opposite direction to affirm faith in Christ.

Repentance is an essential part of the larger experience that we often speak of as conversion. Conversion is a process of transformation through which we become the people God intends us to be. Repentance and conversion must not be limited to any one occasion. Different people experience conversion in different ways. For some, there is

my heart strangely warmed. I felt I did trust in Christ, Christ alone for salvation; and an assurance was given me that he had taken away my sins, even mine, and saved me from the law of sin and death."

The Means by Which God's Grace Comes to Us

Divine grace is made available and effective in human lives through a variety of means or "channels," as Wesley called them. While God is radically free to work in many ways, the Church has been given by God the special responsibility and privilege of being the Body of Christ which carries forth God's purpose of redeeming the world. Wesley recognized the Church itself as a means of grace—a grace-filled and grace-sharing community of faithful people. United Methodism shares with other Protestant communions the understanding that the proclamation of the Word through preaching, teaching, and the life of the Church is a primary means of God's grace. The origin and rapid growth of Methodism as a revival movement occurred largely through the medium of the proclaimed Gospel. John Wesley also emphasized the importance of prayer, fasting, Bible study, and meetings of persons for support and sharing.

Because God has created and is creating all that is, physical objects of creation can become the bearers of divine presence, power, and meaning, and thus become sacramental means of God's grace. Sacraments are effective means of God's presence mediated through the created world.

a moment of change so powerful that forever after they can describe and date the event. For others, conversion is much more gradual; perhaps so much so that they can better look and recognize God's work in their lives than they can identify a specific time and event. We are people with very different personalities and experiences; God honors our differences by dealing with us in diverse ways. It is, then, very important that we never set up our own individual experiences as the standard or test by which those of others are to be judged. For all of us, repentance and conversion must be ongoing throughout our lives. As we grow in faith and trust God in Christ more deeply, we recognize more things in our lives that demand repentance. Our process of conversion needs to involve constant and conscious turning away from sin and turning toward God.

The faith that is necessary for salvation requires us to do something—to surrender our lives in trusting obedience to Christ. But it is important to remember that our ability to have faith is an ability that we have received as a gift from God. We can respond in trusting faith to God's offer of saving grace only because God has already given us this capacity. Faith is not simply knowing or even believing the teachings of Christianity. It is entrusting our lives to Jesus Christ.

There is an old story about a daredevil who was about to ride a bicycle across a tightrope strung over a deep gorge. Seeking encouragement, perhaps, he asked the bystanders if they believed that he could perform this feat successfully. Many of them cheered loudly and affirmed that, indeed, they believed that he could do it. The daredevil then uncovered his bicycle and revealed that it had a second seat. "All right," he said, "who among the believers will ride with me?" To have faith is to trust, to climb aboard, and take a lifelong ride with Christ.

MEANS OF GRACE

God's grace comes to us in many ways. From the natural world around us, we see that God is a lover of beauty; we marvel at the complexity and intricacy of created things. God's grace reaches out to us through other people as they show us glimpses of divine love or sometimes as they hurt us so much that we are driven to seek solace in God. Through the Holy Spirit, God works in us directly, especially as we read the Scriptures, meditate and pray, or otherwise intentionally listen for the divine voice. God's grace is revealed in the diverse experiences of our lives—in the glorious times when we are aware of God with us and in the dark times when it may be only later that we realize we were never alone.

God becoming incarnate in Jesus Christ is the supreme instance of this kind of divine action. Wesley viewed the sacraments as crucial means of grace and affirmed the Anglican teaching "that a sacrament is 'an outward sign of inward grace, and a means whereby we receive the same.'" Combining words, actions, and physical elements, sacraments are sign-acts which both express and convey God's grace and love. Baptism and the Lord's Supper are sacraments that were instituted or commanded by Christ in the Gospels.

United Methodists believe that these sign-acts are special means of grace. The ritual action of a sacrament does not merely point to God's presence in the world, but also participates in it and becomes a vehicle for conveying that reality. God's presence in the sacraments is real, but it must be accepted by human faith if it is to transform human lives. The sacraments do not convey grace either magically or irrevocably, but they are powerful channels through which God has chosen to make grace available to us. Wesley identified baptism as the initiatory sacrament by which we enter into the covenant with God and are admitted as members of Christ's Church. He understood the Lord's Supper as nourishing and empowering the lives of Christians and strongly advocated frequent participation in it. The Wesleyan tradition has continued to practice and cherish the various means through which divine grace is made present to us.

Christians believe the supreme means by which God's grace comes to us is the life, death, and resurrection of Jesus Christ. If a sacrament is understood as a special means of grace, then Christ is the essential and central sacrament. In sacraments God uses physical objects of creation as vehicles of divine love. In the human life of Christ, God made the divine self most available to us.

The church can be understood sacramentally also. As the primary institution designated by God to continue the work of Christ in the world, the church is itself a means of grace. God reaches us through the various ministries of the church—through the proclamation of the Word in preaching and teaching, through worship and music, through the fellowship of other Christians, through concrete acts of compassion, through work toward peace, justice, and liberation. In our baptism we are made a part of this community of faith and offered its ministries as a means by which divine grace works in our lives.

United Methodism has always valued the means of grace. John Wesley taught that the means of grace instituted by Christ were prayer, searching the Scriptures, receiving the Lord's Supper, fasting, and joining with other Christians for mutual nurture and accountability. Wesley stressed the necessity of intentional Christian living and provided directions for Methodist people to follow.

The sacraments of baptism and Holy Communion are special means of grace that God has given us. They are not simply reminders of what Christ has done; they are actual channels through which grace is made available. Because God has chosen to use them, the physical elements of water, bread, and wine (along with the words of the rituals) are sign-acts of divine love. They are a kind of divine "show and tell." God communicates to us on a level that we can understand through the sacraments. But the sacraments do more than just help us to understand God; they also enable us to experience God. As good parents tenderly care for their children by meeting their physical needs, those children, even as infants, begin to grasp what it means to be loved. As we celebrate the sacraments, we experience the tender, loving care of our parent God. In preaching, God's love is made audible; so in the sacraments, God's love is made visible (James F. White, *Introduction to Christian Worship*, p. 170). In baptism we are initiated into the church—the family of God; in the Eucharist we are nourished and sustained in our ongoing journey of faith. Both are precious and powerful means to receive God's grace.

Leader Helps

RESOURCES AND MATERIALS
- Copies of the study guide
- Bibles
- Current magazines and newspapers
- Copies of *The United Methodist Hymnal*

SESSION GUIDE

1. Have the group look together at the two accounts of creation in Genesis 1 and 2 and at the story of the Fall in Genesis 3. Depending upon their familiarity with these Scriptures, read some portions aloud. Emphasize the creative work of God and the goodness of the created order. Examine Genesis 3:7-24 to find the results of sin. With members of the group following along in their Bibles, point out that the first chapters of Genesis are stories revealing the effects of sin upon human beings in general. Then, at the end of chapter 11, the focus narrows to Abraham, Sarah, and their descendants—the family, and eventually nation, chosen as a special divine instrument. Notice Genesis 12:1-3 as the first of many biblical affirmations of the covenant between God and Israel. (Other examples can be found in Isaiah 19:24, 49:6, 51:2; and Romans 4:13.) Note particularly the last part of verse 3 in which the benefits of this special relationship are extended to all nations. Discuss the idea of the Jews as God's chosen people. Strive to make clear that this is not a choice that bestows privilege, but one that demands obedience; it is a relationship through which God reaches out to all people.

2. Share newspaper and magazine clippings that illustrate the reality of sin in its various manifestations. Help the group to realize that the consequences of sin are not simply sensational violence, but rather they are the more subtle expressions of our brokenness. Use examples that make it clear that sin is seen throughout our society, not just in the actions of individuals.

3. The famous theologian Karl Barth was once asked whether or not the serpent in the garden of Eden spoke with an audible voice. His answer is said to have been, "Yes, it still does; I hear it every day." Encourage the group to discuss their own hearing and responding to the voices of evil.

4. Discuss together, or in small groups, the first two questions in paragraph 4 of the "Baptismal Covenant I" (p. 34 of *The United Methodist Hymnal* or p. 53 in the study guide). Ask the participants to reflect upon how they live out the answers to these questions in everyday life. Then ask them to look at the third question in this section. Encourage the group to relate and compare their own experiences of repentance, trust, and conversion. It is important that members of the group understand grace as the free, undeserved, and unearned favor of God. Many Christians struggle to accept the idea that we are completely unable to save ourselves and totally dependent upon the active love of God. Discuss the various ways or means that God's grace is known in our lives. Encourage the sharing of personal experiences.

5. Give each participant a *Hymnal*, and call attention to the section of hymns on prevenient grace (Nos. 337-360). Point out that these hymns are divided (note top right corner of page) into hymns of invitation and repentance. Read portions of No. 337 "Only Trust Him," No. 351 "Pass Me Not, O Gentle Savior," and No. 357 "Just as I Am, Without One Plea." Discuss the meaning of some of these hymns in light of the ideas in this session. Suggest that hymns in this section be used in personal devotional time in the days ahead.

6. Wesley affirmed the traditional Anglican understanding of a sacrament as "an outward sign of inward grace, and a means whereby we receive the same." Discuss the meaning of this definition and how our current understandings of baptism and Holy Communion differ from Wesley's. Look together at paragraph one of the "Baptismal Covenant I." As you discuss its meaning, focus on the verbs: "initiated," "incorporated," "given," "offered."

7. Encourage the participants to read Session Three in preparation for the next session.

TO EXPAND THIS STUDY
- Read and discuss this quotation from *Remember Who You Are* by William H. Willimon:

  ...to ask whether infants and children may be baptized is to ask whether God's grace and salvation are free enough, undeserved enough, unmerited enough, and great enough to include even children. Every time we baptize a baby, we proclaim to all the world that God's grace is sufficient. And it is given freely to all....Faith itself is *God's* gift. Faith happens when I am grasped by God, not when I grope around for God. Where faith is understood as human grasping for God, only adults can be baptized. Where faith is seen as the reception of a gift, infants may be candidates for that gift (pp. 66-67).

- Use Matthew 27:51 to illustrate the truth that the barriers between God and human beings were destroyed by the death of Christ. The curtain divided the most holy place, where the presence of God was believed to be most intense, from the parts of the Temple into which people could go more freely. The most holy place was entered only by the high priest, only on the highest holy day, when he sprinkled the blood of a sacrificial animal on the mercy seat, asking for God's forgiveness of the people's sin. It was a place of mystery, of awe, of terror. But in the death of Christ, God becomes accessible to us; the separation caused by sin is healed.

- Use 2 Corinthians 5:18-20 to begin discussion of the role of the Christian church and of individual Christians in continuing Christ's work in this world.

The Meaning of Baptism

Baptism and the Life of Faith

The New Testament records that Jesus was baptized by John (Matthew 3:13-17) and commanded his disciples to teach and baptize in the name of the Father, Son, and Holy Spirit (Matthew 28:19). Baptism is grounded in the life, death, and resurrection of Jesus Christ; the grace which baptism makes available is that of the atonement of Christ which makes possible our reconciliation with God. Baptism involves dying to sin, newness of life, union with Christ, receiving the Holy Spirit, and incorporation into Christ's Church. United Methodists affirm this understanding in their official documents of faith. Article XVII of the Articles of Religion (Methodist) calls baptism "a sign of regeneration or the new birth;" the Confession of Faith (EUB) states that baptism is "a representation of the new birth in Christ Jesus and a mark of Christian discipleship."

The Baptismal Covenant

In both the Old and New Testament, God enters into covenant relationship with God's people. A covenant involves promises and responsibilities of both parties; it is instituted through a special ceremony and expressed by a distinguishing sign. By covenant God constituted a servant community of the people of Israel,

BIBLICAL ROOTS

Christian baptism has its roots in various Jewish rituals that use water as a sign of cleansing and renewal. When Jesus came to John the Baptist to receive baptism, he was showing that even though without sin himself, he was voluntarily sharing the burden of human sinfulness. His baptism by John marked the beginning of his earthly ministry.

Jesus commanded the disciples then and commands the church now to baptize in the name of God who was made known to us in the life, death, and resurrection of Christ. Probably the earliest Christian baptisms were administered in the name of Jesus only, but soon, as Christians came to better understand the divine nature, baptisms recognized the triune personality of God traditionally expressed as Father, Son, and Holy Spirit.

God has chosen to use the sacrament of baptism as one of the ways that divine love comes to us. The grace offered to us in baptism is grace made available through the work of Jesus Christ. When we receive baptism, the forgiving, cleansing, saving power of God is applied to our individual lives. This is such an important part of God's working with us that the risen Christ, in his last conversation with his disciples, specifically instructed them to baptize.

The word *testament* comes from a Latin term that can also be translated as *covenant*. Therefore, the two major parts of the Bible could be called the Old and New Covenants; indeed, in some English versions these names are used. Our God is a covenant-making God—one who chooses to come into relationship with human beings, a relationship with promises and responsibilities on both sides. The Old Testament is the story of the "old covenant"—the covenant between God and the people of Israel. This covenant was first established when God appeared to Abraham and promised that he would become the father of a great nation, which would serve as an instrument of the divine purpose. The sign of this covenant would be the circumcision of all male members of the community. God reaffirmed the covenant promise to Abraham's descendants—Isaac, Jacob, and Joseph. Over and over, the divine promise is repeated: "I will take you as my people and

promising to be their God and giving them the Law to make clear how they were to live. The circumcision of male infants is the sign of this covenant (Genesis 17:1-14, Exodus 24:1-12). In the death and resurrection of Jesus Christ, God fulfilled the prophecy of a new covenant and called forth the Church as a servant community (Jeremiah 31:31-34, 1 Corinthians 11:23-26). The baptism of infants and adults, both male and female, is the sign of this covenant.

Therefore, United Methodists identify our ritual for baptism as "The Services of the Baptismal Covenant" (*The United Methodist Hymnal*, pages 32-54). In baptism the Church declares that it is bound in covenant to God; through baptism new persons are initiated into that covenant. The covenant connects God, the community of faith, and the person being baptized; all three are essential to the fulfillment of the baptismal covenant. The faithful grace of God initiates the covenant relationship and enables the community and the person to respond with faith.

Baptism by Water and the Holy Spirit

Through the work of the Holy Spirit—the continuing presence of Christ on earth—the Church is instituted to be the community of the new covenant. Within this community, baptism is by water and the Spirit (John 3:5, Acts 2:38). In God's work of salvation, the mystery of Christ's death and resurrection is inseparably linked with the gift of the Holy Spirit given on the day of Pentecost (Acts 2). Likewise, participation in Christ's death and resurrection is inseparably

I will be your God" (Exodus 6:7). Centuries later, God renewed this covenant with Israel after delivering the people from slavery in Egypt. At Mount Sinai, God through Moses made clear that Israel's responsibility in the covenant was to live faithfully according to God's will as expressed in the Law. Making and renewing the covenant were usually expressed in ceremonies in which the whole community participated. These ceremonies frequently involved the symbolic use of blood, which the Israelites understood to be the very essence of life. New members were received into the covenant community through such ceremonies. Males were circumcised to mark them as a part of the community. Male children born to families in the covenant community were circumcised at eight days of age.

Sadly, the effects of human sinfulness proved to be so strong that the people are unable to live up to their side of the covenant. Over and over the cycle is repeated: The people sin by violating God's law; God forgives and rescues them from the plight of sin; the people are unable to remain faithful; they fall again into sin. Much of the Old Testament is the story of this broken covenant. Some of the prophets realized that the very nature of human beings had to be changed if they were ever going to be able to live faithfully in a covenant relationship with God. These prophets spoke of a future time when God would act decisively to make this possible in a new covenant with God's people.

A NEW COVENANT

Christians believe that this promised new covenant was established by the life, death, and resurrection of Jesus Christ. Christ himself makes this explicit when he speaks of the wine at the Last Supper as symbolizing "the new covenant in my blood" (Luke 22:20). Throughout the history of the church, baptism has been understood as the sign of this new covenant. Baptism is the ceremony that identifies people of all ages as participants in this covenant between God and humankind. In accord with the Christian gospel's affirmation of the equal value of all people before God, the sign of the new covenant is offered to both males and females.

The use of the title "Baptismal Covenant" is a return to an earlier practice in Methodism. This title is an important expression of our understanding of baptism as the occasion when an individual is incorporated into the community of faith.

Just as Israel is a community in covenant relationship with God since the time of Abraham, the Christian church is the community of the new covenant established in and through Jesus Christ. Through the presence of the Holy Spirit, God

linked with receiving the Spirit (Romans 6:1-11, 8:9-14). The Holy Spirit who is the power of creation (Genesis 1:2) is also the giver of new life. Working in the lives of people before, during, and after their baptism, the Spirit is the effective agent of salvation. God bestows upon baptized persons the presence of the Holy Spirit, marks them with an identifying seal as God's own, and implants in their hearts the first installment of their inheritance as sons and daughters of God (2 Corinthians 1:21-22). It is through the Spirit that the life of faith is nourished until the final deliverance when they will enter into the fullness of salvation (Ephesians 1:13-14).

Since the Apostolic Age, baptism by water and baptism of the Holy Spirit have been connected (Acts 19:17). Christians are baptized with both, sometimes by different sign-actions. Water is administered in the name of the triune God (specified in the ritual as Father, Son, and Holy Spirit) by an authorized person and the Holy Spirit is invoked with the laying on of hands, in the presence of the congregation. Water provides the central symbolism for baptism. The richness of its meaning for the Christian community is suggested in the baptismal liturgy which speaks of the waters of creation and the flood, the liberation of God's people by passage through the sea, the gift of water in the wilderness, and the passage through the Jordan River to the promised land. In baptism we identify ourselves with this people of God and join the community's journey toward God. The use of water in baptism also symbolizes cleansing from sin, death to old life,

continues the work of Christ in overcoming the effects of sin and bringing the world back into reconciled relationship with God.

WATER AND SPIRIT

Christian baptism is by water and the Spirit. Water plays a major part in the biblical story of God and God's people. In the acts of creation, God's Spirit moved over and acted upon the waters; the first animal life came forth from the water (Genesis 1:1-10 and 20-21). It has been suggested that this is one reason why the fish became an early symbol of Christianity. As it was from water that physical life began, so it is from water that every human life comes into existence. The nourishing and protecting waters of the mother's womb flow out as a new child enters the world. Some early baptismal fonts were shaped to resemble wombs to portray baptism as the sacrament of new life. In the conversation between Jesus and Nicodemus in John 3:1-8, spiritual birth is said to be by water and the Spirit. In contrast, water in the Scripture is also associated with death, as it is, of course, in our own experience. Interestingly, many early baptismal fonts were also made to look like tombs to portray baptism as a kind of dying. The story of the great Flood in Genesis 6-9 shows God's use of water to destroy sin. Yet even in the midst of so much death by water, God rescued Noah, his family, and specimens of animals so that the earth might be repopulated and life continue. The ark, the vehicle through which life was preserved, appropriately became and remains a symbol for the Christian church. In Romans 6:1-11, Paul describes baptism as dying to sin and rising with Christ. Even from the water of death, there comes new life.

Other biblical accounts associate water with other salvation themes present in baptism. The Hebrew people were freed from their slavery in Egypt by God's action, which enabled them to escape through the sea (Exodus 14:19-31). So, baptism is liberation from sin. As they wandered in the wilderness, God provided water to keep the Hebrews alive (Exodus 17:1-7 and Numbers 20:2-11). Baptism is not limited to a moment in time, but is God's promise to sustain our spiritual life. By following God's direction, the people of Israel eventually cross the Jordan River into the land that God had promised them (Joshua 3:7-17). In John's vision of the heavenly city where God's purpose is finally fulfilled, there is the spring and a river "of the water of life" (Revelation 21:6, 22:1). Baptism is God's action to fulfill the divine promise of salvation.

In all of these biblical passages, the Holy Spirit is involved as the active presence of God working to carry out the divine will and plan. In some instances the work of the Spirit is simply

and rising to begin new life in Christ. In United Methodist tradition, the water of baptism may be administered by sprinkling, pouring, or immersion. However it is administered, water should be utilized with enough generosity to enhance our appreciation of its symbolic meanings.

The baptismal liturgy includes the biblical symbol of the anointing with the Holy Spirit—the laying on of hands with the optional use of oil. This anointing promises to the baptized person the power to live faithfully the kind of life that water baptism signifies. In the early centuries of the Church, the laying on of hands usually followed immediately upon administration of the water and completed the ritual of membership. Because the laying on of hands was, in the Western Church, an act to be performed only by a bishop, it was later separated from water baptism and came to be called confirmation. In confirmation the Holy Spirit marked the baptized person as God's own and strengthened him or her for discipleship. In the worship life of the early Church, the water and the anointing led directly to the celebration of the Lord's Supper as part of the service of initiation, regardless of the age of the baptized. The current rituals of the Baptismal Covenant rejoin these three elements into a unified service. Together these symbols point to, anticipate, and offer participation in the life of the community of faith as it embodies God's presence in the world.

assumed, but in others the Spirit's role is plainly identified. In the Creation account in Genesis 1, it is the Spirit of God that moves over the waters. As the flood is receding, a dove—always a symbol of the Holy Spirit in the Scriptures—brings Noah a sign of life returning. This symbol of the Spirit appears again in the Gospel accounts of the baptism of Christ. The cloud by day and pillar of fire by night that guide Israel through the wilderness are visible forms of the Spirit's presence. God is working in the life of God's covenant community by water and the spirit.

This discussion of the significance of water reminds us of the confusion and, sometimes, the disagreements about how water is to be used in baptism, and what quantity of it is needed. Throughout our history, Methodism has offered adults and parents of infants the choice of three modes—sprinkling, pouring, and immersion. In the absence of scriptural information on the subject, we believe that baptisms in the early church were probably conducted in a variety of styles. Although it is common among some groups to insist that Jesus was baptized by immersion, there is no clear evidence to this effect. Descriptions of Jesus and others going into or coming out of the water may simply refer to their stepping off from and back onto the shore. Indeed, the very early use of a shell as a symbol of baptism offers evidence that water may have been poured over the head of an individual who was standing in or being held over water. All three traditional modes have rich symbolic value. Sprinkling expresses both the imagery of cleansing (Ezekiel 36:25-27) and of setting apart for service to God (Exodus 29:21). Pouring expresses the outpouring of the Holy Spirit upon the person being baptized and upon the whole church (Acts 2:1-4, 17-18). Immersion expresses dying to sin and rising to new life, participation in the death and resurrection of Christ (Romans 6:1-11 and Colossians 2:11-12). The rich symbolism of water as discussed above can be most meaningfully experienced if water is used in ways and amounts that allow it to be seen and heard. This can be done with any mode of baptism.

The work of the Holy Spirit in baptism is signified by the laying on of hands and the anointing with oil. Both of these actions have roots in both the Old and New Testaments. The laying on of hands was a biblical symbol of consecration for an office or service and was understood to convey divine authorization and empowerment. (See Numbers 8:10-11; 27:18-23; Acts 6:5-6, 13:2-3 for examples.) In addition to the use of this action in baptism, United Methodist bishops lay hands upon people being ordained as clergy. Anointing with oil is less common in our tradition, but it has a powerful symbolic significance, one which we ought to recover. In the

Baptism as Incorporation into the Body of Christ

Christ constitutes the Church as his Body by the power of the Holy Spirit (1 Corinthians 12:13, 27). The Church draws new persons into itself as it seeks to remain faithful to its commission to proclaim and exemplify the Gospel. Baptism is the sacrament of initiation and incorporation into the Body of Christ. An infant, child, or adult who is baptized becomes a member of the catholic (universal) Church, of the denomination, and of the local congregation. Therefore, baptism is a rite of the whole Church which ordinarily requires the participation of the gathered, worshiping congregation. In a series of promises within the liturgy of baptism, the community affirms its own faith and pledges to act as spiritual mentor and support for the one who is baptized. Baptism is not merely an individualistic, private, or domestic occasion. When unusual but legitimate circumstances prevent a baptism from taking place in the midst of the gathered community during its regular worship, every effort should be made to assemble representatives of the congregation to participate in the celebration. Later, the baptism should be recognized in the public assembly of worship in order that the congregation may make its appropriate affirmations of commitment and responsibility.

Baptism brings us into union with Christ, with each other, and with the Church in every time and place.

Bible, oil is a symbol of the Holy Spirit. In the Old Testament, priests and kings were anointed with oil as a sign of their call by God into a special role; even objects were anointed to designate them as holy. (See Exodus 30:22-38 and 1 Samuel 16:1-13 for examples.) In the New Testament, anointing was a sign of healing (Mark 6:13 and James 5:14), of hospitality and love (Luke 7:36-50), and of the claiming and equipping by the Spirit (2 Corinthians 1:21-22 and 1 John 2:20, 27).

In the practice of the church for centuries, baptism with water, laying on of hands with anointing, and receiving the elements of Holy Communion were all combined in one service of Christian initiation, regardless of the age of the person being initiated. While the churches of Eastern Orthodoxy retained this practice, the Roman Catholic Church and the Protestant churches that developed out of it did not. The change in practice was not the result of intentional theological decision, but rather an accidental, practical development. The Roman Catholic, Anglican, and other churches in western Europe insisted that the laying on of hands with anointing could only be performed by a bishop. As the churches grew in numbers and spread out geographically, long delays occurred between baptism by a priest or pastor and a visit by a bishop. This delay in receiving the laying on of hands with anointing meant postponement of participation in Holy Communion. (More will be said about this in Session Five when we discuss confirmation.) The baptismal rituals of our present hymnal have reunited these aspects of Christian initiation into one service.

INCORPORATION INTO THE BODY OF CHRIST

Baptism brings people into the church—the body of Christ. To speak of the church in this way is to affirm that it is more than a human organization. The church is the instrument chosen by God to continue the work of Christ on earth. It functions as his Body—his arms, his hands, his feet, and so on—by doing the tasks that God has assigned it. Further, as the physical body is made up of diverse members with differing functions, so is the church. The body of Christ is a community of faith, a family of God, composed of people who are in close fellowship with each other and with Christ.

The church initiates and incorporates new members through the sacrament of baptism. By receiving baptism, people have participated in the ritual of initiation. They are members of the "catholic," or universal, church of Jesus Christ—the body of Christ made up of all Christians, members of The United Methodist Church—a denomination comprising a portion of the universal church, and members of their local church—a part of both The United Methodist Church and the church universal. In paragraph 16 of the "Baptismal Covenant I" the

Through this sign and seal of our common discipleship, our equality in Christ is made manifest (Galatians 3:27-28). We affirm that there is one baptism into Christ, celebrated as our basic bond of unity in the many communions that make up the Body of Christ (Ephesians 4:4-6). The power of the Spirit in baptism does not depend upon the mode by which water is administered, the age or psychological disposition of the baptized person, or the character of the minister. It is God's grace that makes the sacrament whole. One baptism calls the various churches to overcome their divisions and visibly manifest their unity. Our oneness in Christ calls for mutual recognition of baptism in these communions as a means of expressing the unity that Christ intends (1 Corinthians 12:12-13).

Baptism as Forgiveness of Sin

In baptism God offers and we accept the forgiveness of our sin (Acts 2:38). With the pardoning of sin which has separated us from God, we are justified—freed from the guilt and penalty of sin and restored to right relationship with God. This reconciliation is made possible through the atonement of Christ and made real in our lives by the work of the Holy Spirit. We respond by confessing and repenting of our sin, and affirming our faith that Jesus Christ has accomplished all that is necessary for our salvation. Faith is the necessary condition for justification; in baptism, that faith is professed. God's forgiveness makes possible the renewal of our spiritual lives and our becoming new beings in Christ.

congregation welcomes new people as members of "the body of Christ and in this congregation of The United Methodist Church."

Because the church is a community rather than a collection of separate individuals, baptism is not a private ceremony or simply a personal transaction between an individual and Christ (although, as will be discussed in Session Five, a personal relationship with Christ must be professed). The sacrament proclaims the good news of Christ to the whole church. Therefore, the appropriate occasion for baptism is within a service of public, corporate worship. Most often this will be the regular Sunday worship service of the congregation.

Because The United Methodist Church is only one part of the larger body of Christ, baptism also makes one a member of the universal church. Although there are differences between various groups in baptismal theology and practice, most Christians recognize our fundamental unity in Christ. United Methodists are continuing to work with other Christians through efforts such as the National Council of the Churches of Christ in the USA, the World Council of Churches, and the Consultation on Church Union. Our hope is that we can learn to love and appreciate each other and that eventually there will be fulfillment of the prayer of Christ "that they may all be one" (John 17:20-23).

SIN AND REPENTANCE

The Bible teaches that sin is a condition, not simply a list of certain acts that we call "sins." Sin is the inevitable state or circumstance in which our lives are lived. Only God's forgiveness can free us from the guilt and punishment of sin. God's gracious forgiveness, made available to us through Christ, comes to us in baptism. This grace covers more than the personal sins that have been committed prior to receiving the sacrament. We continue to sin throughout our lives and are continually in need of pardon. Baptism signifies that God's forgiveness is always and repeatedly available to us when we repent.

The first question in the baptismal ritual (paragraph 4) asks for a statement of repentance. Throughout the ritual, there are affirmations of divine forgiveness. Sometimes people are confused about how these references to sin are to be understood when infants are being baptized. The questions in paragraph 4 are, however, addressed to the parents or sponsors. These adults are speaking for themselves; they are not answering for their children. The sad reality is that infants are born into a broken and sinful world alienated from God. They cannot escape the evil influences of this world. As they mature, they

Baptism as New Life

Baptism is the sacramental sign of new life through and in Christ by the power of the Holy Spirit. Variously identified as regeneration, new birth, and being born again, this work of grace makes us into new spiritual creatures (2 Corinthians 5:17). We die to our old nature which was dominated by sin and enter into the very life of Christ who transforms us. Baptism is the means of entry into new life in Christ (John 3:5; Titus 3:5), but new birth may not always coincide with the moment of the administration of water or the laying on of hands. Our awareness and acceptance of our redemption by Christ and new life in him may vary throughout our lives. But, in whatever way the reality of the new birth is experienced, it carries out the promises God made to us in our baptism.

Baptism and Holy Living

New birth into life in Christ, which is signified by baptism, is the beginning of that process of growth in grace and holiness through which God brings us into closer relationship with Jesus Christ, and shapes our lives increasingly into conformity with the divine will. Sanctification is a gift of the gracious presence of the Holy Spirit, a yielding to the Spirit's power, a deepening of our love for God and neighbor. Holiness of heart and life, in the Wesleyan tradition, always involves both personal and social holiness.

Baptism is the doorway to the sanctified life. The sacrament teaches us to live in the expectation of further gifts of God's grace. It initiates us into a community of faith that prays for holiness; it calls us to life lived in faith-

will commit personal sins for which they need pardon. The grace of God received in baptism will continue to make this possible throughout their lives.

Justification is another term for pardon or forgiveness. In other contexts the word is used in reference to the act of carpenters lining up boards so that their angles are correct or to typists spacing lines of print properly. When we are justified we are "moved to the correct position"; we are put in a right relationship with God.

God's forgiveness of sin is to be accepted in faith. When an adult or youth is baptized, that individual professes faith as a part of the ritual, specifically in answer to the third question in paragraph 4. When an infant or young child is baptized, the parents or sponsors profess their own faith; the baptized will make his or her own profession of faith later in life. In both cases, the congregation professes the faith of the church by answering the questions in paragraph 8 and joining in the Apostles' Creed in paragraph 9.

The grace of God, which comes to us through baptism, not only forgives our sins, but makes us into new spiritual beings. We acknowledge the necessity of this when we speak of being born again, born anew, born from above, born spiritually, and other such terms. Without this change in our sinful nature, we would immediately return to our old bondage in sin. In one of the best-loved of Charles Wesley's hymns, "O For a Thousand Tongues to Sing," he praises Christ by saying, "He breaks the power of canceled sin, he sets the prisoner free." It is only by being made into new creatures that we can enjoy new life in a restored and reconciled relationship to God. John Wesley spoke of justification as "what God *does for* us through his Son" and of new life as what God "*works in* us by his Spirit" (from "Justification by Faith," 5:56). In other words, we are not only in a different relationship with God, but we are beginning to be new people. This new spiritual life is our sharing in the very life of the resurrected Christ. It is eternal life—a quality of life that begins now and continues through eternity.

A JOURNEY OF HOLINESS

The physical birth of an infant is not an end in itself; it is the beginning of a process toward maturity. Similarly, spiritual birth is the beginning of a lifelong journey of growth in grace and holiness of life. Salvation is not so much an event as a journey; it is dynamic, not static. God does not simply forgive our sin; God does not only give us new life; God also shapes us into the people God has created us to be. John Wesley wrote that repentance is "the porch of religion," faith is "the

fulness to God's gift. Baptized believers and the community of faith are obligated to manifest to the world the new redeemed humanity which lives in loving relationship with God and strives to put an end to all human estrangements. There are no conditions of human life that exclude persons from the sacrament of baptism. We strive for and look forward to the reign of God on earth, of which baptism is a sign. Baptism is fulfilled only when the believer and the Church are wholly conformed to the image of Christ.

door," and holiness is "religion itself" ("Works," 8:472). This process of growth in holiness is called sanctification. It is carried out by the activity of the Holy Spirit working in our lives to make us more like Jesus Christ.

Sanctification, or holiness, is a gift of divine grace, but it also requires human cooperation. We are responsible for utilizing the various means of grace available to us. As individuals and as a community of faith, we are to open ourselves increasingly to the divine power to show us our sin, to rid our lives of its effects, and to cultivate those qualities of life that make up authentic Christian character. Holiness involves our personal relationship with God—sometimes called the vertical aspect of Christian living—and our social relationships with other people—the horizontal aspect. It is only when both of these aspects are transformed that our lives are truly Christlike—"cruciform" or shaped in the image of the crucified Christ. Personal piety is to be manifested in action for peace and justice. Christians who know Christ as Savior and Lord work to change the conditions of society that make others victims of discrimination, oppression, and poverty. John Wesley made this clear when he wrote: "The gospel of Christ knows of no religion, but social; no holiness but social holiness" ("Works," 14:321).

God is not finished with us until the command of Christ is fulfilled—that we be "perfect...as your heavenly Father is perfect" (Matthew 5:48). Wesley believed that this could happen, not because he thought that we are such good people, but because he knew that God is so great. God is both able and willing to transform us. The goal is that love become "the sole principle of action," that we are motivated by nothing else than the love of God and neighbor.

Leader Helps

RESOURCES AND MATERIALS
- Copies of the study guide
- Bibles
- Copies of *The United Methodist Hymnal*
- Copies of *The Book of Discipline*
- Chalkboard or newsprint
- Chalk or felt-tip markers

SESSION GUIDE

1. Ask the participants to read the section "Biblical Roots" on page 17 and the sections entitled "Baptism and the Life of Faith" and "The Baptismal Covenant" in *By Water and the Spirit*. Then read and discuss the account of Jesus' baptism by John as recorded in Matthew 3:13-17. Note the parallel stories in Mark 1:9-11 and Luke 3:21-22. Provide a brief summary of the role of John the Baptist, emphasizing that he was a "bridge" between the prophets of the Old Testament and the Christian community of the New Testament. Chapters 1 and 3 of Luke will be especially helpful.

2. Have the participants examine and discuss Article XVII from "The Articles of Religion" and the second and third paragraphs of Article VI from "The Confession of Faith." These excerpts from *The Book of Discipline* are reprinted on page 57. Use the following questions to stimulate discussion:
   - What images come to your mind when you hear the words *regeneration, inner cleansing,* and *new birth*?
   - What difference does it make in your life to understand baptism as a "mark of Christian discipleship"?

3. Look together at paragraph 9 (p. 54) of the "Baptismal Covenant I," noting the threefold structure of the profession of faith. Make the group aware that this question and answer form was the way that the creed was used in early Christian baptism. The person being baptized would receive the water (either by immersion, pouring, or sprinkling) after each answer. Note what is called the "Trinitarian baptismal formula" in paragraph 11—"in the name of the Father, and of the Son, and the Holy Spirit." Here the triune nature of God is proclaimed. While this is not the place for a distracting discussion of this controversial issue, the concern throughout the church today is that this formula portrays God in masculine terms. Emphasize that Christians recognize God as neither male nor female and both genders as in the image of God, but that our language makes the expression of this difficult.

4. Study together paragraph 10 (p. 54) of the "Baptismal Covenant I." This portion of the ritual is often called the "flood prayer"; it is comparable to the Great Thanksgiving in the service of Holy Communion. Call attention to the importance of water in the events of salvation history mentioned. Ask the participants to recall ways that they have seen the images of water used in services of baptism or other worship services.

5. Ask the group to look through the baptismal ritual and list on newsprint (or a chalkboard) the points at which there are references to sin and to forgiveness, or cleansing from sin.

6. Read the section "Water and Spirit" on page 19 and the section "Baptism by Water and the Holy Spirit" in *By Water and the Spirit*. Tell the participants that in John Wesley's sermon "The Great Privilege of Those That Are Born of God," he speaks of "...a vast inward change, a change wrought in the soul, by the operation of the Holy Ghost; a change in the whole manner of our existence; for, from the moment we are born of God, we live in quite another manner than we did before; we are, as it were, in another world" (19:224). Have the group discuss this quotation focusing on the ways they experience the Holy Spirit in their lives.

7. Read the sections "Incorporation into the Body of Christ" and "A Journey of Holiness" on pages 21 and 23, and the sections in *By Water and the Spirit* from "Baptism as Incorporation into the Body of Christ" through "Baptism and Holy Living." Point out that The United Methodist Church recognizes the necessity of providing ongoing support and encouragement in members' lifelong journey of holy living. Have the participants read ¶¶ 218 and 219 of *The Book of Discipline* (reprinted on p. 57). Ask them to reflect on the ways that their congregation helps members to "shoulder the burdens, share the risks, and celebrate the joys of fellow members" (¶ 218).

8. Lead the group in talking about the nature of faith as revealed in this practice in the ancient church: Candidates for baptism or the parents of infants to be baptized would knock on the closed outer door of the church. When asked by the priest, "What do you seek of the church?", they would answer "Faith" and then be admitted to receive the sacrament. Ask the participants to consider what their answer would be if they were asked "What do you seek of the church?"

9. Encourage the participants to read Session Four in preparation for the next session.

TO EXPAND THIS STUDY

- Call attention to Romans 6:3-11 and 8:1-17 as passages that help us to understand more deeply the meaning of baptism. Discuss this as much as time allows, but especially encourage the use of these Scriptures for personal study and meditation.

- If questions about the mode of baptism are important concerns of your group, additional Scripture passages for consideration may be found in *The United Methodist Book of Worship*, page 81.

- Lead the group in reading and discussing selected portions of the Old Testament in which the concept of covenant is presented. Suggested passages include the call of Abraham in Genesis 12:1-3; the account of an ancient covenant-making ceremony in Genesis 15:1-21; and the institution of the practice of circumcision as the sign of the covenant in Genesis 17. For the continuation of the covenant and the giving of divine law as Israel's responsibility, see Exodus 19:1-6 and 20:1-17. The importance of blood in covenant making is illustrated in Exodus 24. Traces of this idea are found in our saying that something binding is "written in blood" and the concept of "blood brothers." Jeremiah 31:31-34 contains a beautiful promise of the new covenant. Discuss how this covenant is to be different from the old. Examine 1 Corinthians 11:23-26, noting how Jesus spoke of the shedding of his blood on the cross as signifying the establishment of a new covenant.

- For many Christians the Holy Spirit remains something of a dull blur, a third person of the Trinity often referred to as "it," little understood or

appreciated. If this appears to be true of your group, consider using Chapter V of a denominational classic—*Major United Methodist Beliefs* by Bishop Mack B. Stokes.

- Share with the group the first paragraph of the introduction to the Services of the Baptismal Covenant in *The Book of Worship* (p. 81). Point out that the rituals for Holy Communion, marriage, and death and resurrection are to be used within services of public, corporate worship. All of these are indicators of the recovery of the significance of the body of Christ in United Methodism.

- Use the first paragraph on page 32 of *The United Methodist Hymnal* to encourage discussion of baptism as incorporating people into the community of the new covenant.

- Today's United Methodists are often rather reluctant to speak about being born again or spiritually reborn. This is probably because of occasional overly simplistic uses of these terms or, in some cases, disturbing expressions of judgmental arrogance on the part of people who use them freely. We should not, however, allow misuse of such language to keep us from an appreciation of the truth that God's grace not only forgives our sins, but also makes us into new people. Use the following passages to encourage discussion of this concept: John 3:1-10, 2 Corinthians 5:17, and 1 Peter 1:3-5.

- Use this quote from *Baptism, Eucharist and Ministry* (Geneva: World Council of Churches, 1982) as the basis for a discussion of the relationship between baptism and Christian unity: "Through baptism, Christians are brought into union with Christ, with each other and with the Church of every time and place. Our common baptism, which unites us to Christ in faith, is thus a basic bond of unity....Therefore, our one baptism into Christ constitutes a call to the churches to overcome their divisions and visibly manifest their fellowship" (p. 3).

- Use *A Place for Baptism* by Regina Kuehn (Chicago: Liturgy Training Publications, 1992) as a visual resource to expand participants' horizons about the size, shape, and location of baptismal fonts and pools. Ask all to share what significance such features have or might have for people.

SESSION FOUR—
The Baptism
of Infants and Adults

Baptism as God's Gift to Persons of Any Age

There is one baptism as there is one source of salvation—the gracious love of God. The baptizing of a person, whether as an infant or an adult, is a sign of God's saving grace. That grace—experienced by us as initiating, enabling, and empowering—is the same for all persons. All stand in need of it and none can be saved without it. The difference between the baptism of adults and that of infants is that the Christian faith is consciously being professed by an adult who is baptized. A baptized infant comes to profess her or his faith later in life, after having been nurtured and taught by parent(s) or other responsible adults and the community of faith. Infant baptism is the prevailing practice in situations where children are born to believing parents and brought up in Christian homes and communities of faith. Adult baptism is the norm when the Church is in a missionary situation, reaching out to persons in a culture which is indifferent or hostile to the faith. While the baptism of infants is appropriate for Christian families, the increasingly minority status of the Church in contemporary society demands more attention to evangelizing, nurturing, and baptizing adult converts.

SACRAMENTAL UNDERSTANDING

John Wesley defined a sacrament as "an outward sign of an inward grace, and a means whereby we receive the same" (from "The Means of Grace," 16:188). Regardless of the age of the person being baptized, the active agent in the sacrament is God. Divine grace comes to those who are baptized. The traditions that have joined together to form The United Methodist Church have always offered baptism to people of any age, from infants to the elderly. God's grace is available for all; one can never be too young or too old to both need and receive it. It is appropriate that different people are baptized at different points in their lives. A child who is born in a Christian family and will be brought up within the nurturing community of the church should be baptized as an infant. That child's own profession of faith in Christ will take place later in life when he or she is competent to make such decisions.

ADULT BAPTISM

An adult who has grown up outside of the community of faith and, therefore, has never been baptized should receive the sacrament when he or she is ready to profess faith in Christ. Adult baptisms are most common in situations where the Christian faith is being proclaimed for the first time. This is why most baptisms mentioned in the New Testament are baptisms of adults. These people were being converted to faith in Christ from the non-Christian world. Adult baptism continued to be the common practice as the gospel has been carried to various parts of the world through mission efforts. In the late years of the twentieth century, society is increasingly secular. Our period of history is often called the "post-Christian" era. The church is again in a missionary situation and must attend seriously to the conversion of adults who were either not raised in Christian homes and churches or who have rejected their Christian identity as they grew up. Such adults need to be carefully taught and nurtured. A new resource is now available to guide this process in United Methodism. It was written by Daniel Benedict and is entitled *Come to the Waters: Baptism and Our Ministry of Welcoming Seekers and Making Disciples.* Through the use of such material, pastors and congregations can help adults prepare to commit themselves to Christian discipleship and be baptized or, if they have been previously baptized, to reaffirm their commitment. Of course,

Infant baptism has been the historic practice of the overwhelming majority of the Church throughout the Christian centuries. While the New Testament contains no explicit mandate, there is ample evidence for the baptism of infants in Scripture (Acts 2:38-41, 16:15,33), and in early Christian doctrine and practice. Infant baptism rests firmly on the understanding that God prepares the way of faith before we request or even know that we need help (prevenient grace). The sacrament is a powerful expression of the reality that all persons come before God as no more than helpless infants, unable to do anything to save ourselves, dependent upon the grace of our loving God. The faithful covenant community of the Church serves as a means of grace for those whose lives are impacted by its ministry. Through the Church, God claims infants as well as adults to be participants in the gracious covenant of which baptism is the sign. This understanding of the workings of divine grace also applies to persons who for reasons of handicapping conditions or other limitations are unable to answer for themselves the questions of the baptismal ritual. While we may not be able to comprehend how God works in their lives, our faith teaches us that God's grace is sufficient for their needs and, thus, they are appropriate recipients of baptism.

The Church affirms that children being born into the brokenness of the world should receive the cleansing and renewing forgiveness of God no less than adults. The saving grace made available through Christ's atonement is the only hope of salvation for persons of any age. In baptism infants enter baptism is far from the conclusion of an adult's journey of faith. She or he anticipates future growth in holiness and committed discipleship.

INFANT BAPTISM

When I was growing up as a Methodist in a very small town in eastern North Carolina, I was occasionally challenged by my Baptist friends to justify what they considered to be the rather odd practice of baptizing infants. We Methodists and Presbyterians were a small minority group in the midst of a heavily Baptist population. I really grew up believing that infant baptism was something done by a few churches who, for whatever reason, had decided to be different from everybody else. As I have had opportunity to learn something of the history of Christianity, I have realized that it was the Baptists whose practice needed to be defended. Infant baptism is the ancient and almost universal practice of the church, beginning probably in the New Testament period. Only a few groups, such as Baptists and Disciples of Christ, limit baptism to adults.

In a very powerful way, it is in the baptism of an infant that we most authentically represent how God works in our lives toward salvation. While older people may believe that they are capable of contributing to their own salvation, the sad truth is that all of us are helpless in becoming the people God wants us to be; we are utterly dependent upon divine grace. The glorious, joyful truth is that God loves us and takes the action necessary to bring us into a reconciled relationship with God. This we see most clearly when the person receiving baptism is an infant, plainly incapable of doing anything for himself or herself.

In this way, the baptism of people of any age is alike: It is a sign and means of God's grace. For the same reason, people whose physical and/or mental condition is such that they cannot profess faith for themselves are eligible for baptism, just as they are eligible for God's love. The difference between adult believers' baptism and infant baptism is that adults are capable of rejecting divine grace. Therefore, adults must come to the sacrament having made decisions of repentance and faith. The baptism of an infant looks beyond the moment of the event toward later fulfillment in repentance and faith.

The baptism of an infant is an early step in that individual's lifelong journey of faith—a beginning, not an ending. It is essential that the maturing child be carefully nurtured in spiritual development and intentionally taught about the Christian faith and the life of discipleship. Otherwise, the baptismal grace will be like seeds sown on stony ground; it will not

into a new life in Christ as children of God and members of the Body of Christ. The baptism of an infant incorporates him or her into the community of faith and nurture, including membership in the local church.

The baptism of infants is properly understood and valued if the child is loved and nurtured by the faithful worshiping church and by the child's own family. If a parent or sponsor (godparent) cannot or will not nurture the child in the faith, then baptism is to be postponed until Christian nurture is available. A child who dies without being baptized is received into the love and presence of God because the Spirit has worked in that child to bestow saving grace. If a child has been baptized but her or his family or sponsors do not faithfully nurture the child in the faith, the congregation has a particular responsibility for incorporating the child into its life.

Understanding the practice as an authentic expression of how God works in our lives, The United Methodist Church strongly advocates the baptism of infants within the faith community: "Because the redeeming love of God, revealed in Jesus Christ, extends to all persons and because Jesus explicitly included the children in his kingdom, the pastor of each charge shall earnestly exhort all Christian parents or guardians to present their children to the Lord in Baptism at an early age" (1992 *Book of Discipline*, par. 221). We affirm that while thanksgiving to God and dedication of parents to the task of Christian child raising are aspects of infant baptism, the sacrament is primarily a gift of divine grace. Neither parents or infants are the chief

develop and grow. Therefore, infant baptism is appropriate only for children who will be raised and nurtured as Christians. Usually this means having at least one Christian parent, although there are circumstances in which this role will be assumed by a grandparent, guardian, or other Christian adult.

If there is no likelihood that the faith process of which baptism is a part will be continued in the child's life, baptism is best postponed. The child may be baptized later if changed circumstances mean that Christian nurture will be given or when he or she is sufficiently mature to profess his or her own faith. Pastors face difficult situations when they are asked to baptize a child when there is no evidence that the child will be raised as a Christian. Usually such requests come out of parents' misunderstanding of the significance of baptism. Often pastors can respond to such situations with loving concern by having an honest discussion with parents. The best resource for such a conversation is the baptismal ritual itself. Sharing with parents the serious significance of the vows that they will be taking before God and the church will often result in a sobering appreciation of what they are undertaking when their infant is baptized. Some will sadly realize that they cannot affirm such vows with integrity. Our prayerful hope is that they will be motivated to open themselves to the transforming power of the Holy Spirit.

Unfortunately, there may be occasions when parents (or other adults) persist in asking for the baptism of an infant under circumstances that in the prayerful judgment of the pastor are inappropriate. In such painful cases, the pastor should refuse to offer the sacrament until those circumstances have changed. It is vastly preferable to avoid such situations if possible. Often this can be done by conscientious preaching, teaching, and counseling about the meaning of baptism as a regular part of one's ministry. If people in congregations understand what the sacrament is and does, they are much less likely to approach it lightly. The use of such a resource as *By Water and the Spirit* should yield rich dividends in this regard. Pastors should be greatly aided by the adoption of an official interpretive statement on baptism for The United Methodist Church. Congregations may wish to develop a written statement outlining the meaning of baptism and the church's procedures for its practice.

The current *Book of Discipline*, like its predecessors, makes clear that it is the duty of Christian parents to have their infant children baptized and the duty of pastors to "earnestly exhort" them to do so. The United Methodist Church does not offer infant dedication as a substitute for baptism. The sharp contrast between the two services was well expressed by the actors; baptism is an act of God in and through the Church.

We respect the sincerity of parents who choose not to have their infants baptized, but we acknowledge that these views do not coincide with the Wesleyan understanding of the nature of the sacrament. The United Methodist Church does not accept either the idea that only believer's baptism is valid or the notion that the baptism of infants magically imparts salvation apart from active personal faith. Pastors are instructed by the *Book of Discipline* to explain our teaching clearly on these matters, so that parent(s) or sponsors might be free of misunderstandings.

The United Methodist Book of Worship contains "An Order of Thanksgiving for the Birth or Adoption of the Child" (pages 585-87), which may be recommended in situations where baptism is inappropriate, but parents wish to take responsibility publicly for the growth of the child in faith. It should be made clear that this rite is in no way equivalent to or a substitute for baptism. Neither is it an act of infant dedication. If the infant has not been baptized, the sacrament should be administered as soon as possible after the Order of Thanksgiving.

God's Faithfulness to the Baptismal Covenant

Since baptism is primarily an act of God in the Church, the sacrament is to be received by an individual only once. This position is in accord with the historic teaching of the Church universal, originating as early as the second century and having been recently reaffirmed ecumenically in *Baptism, Eucharist and Ministry*.

Commission on Worship, which prepared the ritual for the 1964 *Book of Hymns*: "In a dedication we make a gift of a life to God for him to accept; in a sacrament God offers the gift of his unfailing grace for us to accept." Certainly there is an element of dedication present in infant baptism as parents or sponsors pledge to raise the child in the faith. The sacrament, however, has additional and richer meaning; it must not be reduced to a solely human action.

Another confusing term in our understanding of infant baptism is "christening." Of the numerous and varied groups of United Methodists with whom I have had the opportunity to discuss baptism, this question has been asked in every one. Obviously, and sadly, this term has been widely used by pastors as well as laypeople in an attempt to represent infant baptism as something different from and less than "the real thing." There is and never has been an official service of christening distinct from baptism in the churches that comprise United Methodism. The only appropriate use of the term is as a synonym for baptism; they are one and the same. The word "christen" may be a carryover of the word *chrism,* which refers to the anointing oil used in baptism or a derivative of the English word "Christianize" meaning to make one a member of the church. Today, it is much better to omit the term "christening" from usage since it only encourages confusion and adds nothing to our understanding of the sacrament.

When Christian parents misunderstand baptism as a human action, rather than the act of God through the church, and choose not to have their child baptized, pastors and teachers have the responsibility to explain, in the spirit of loving concern, our church's position on the sacrament. While no parent should be pressured or encouraged to have a child baptized for inappropriate reasons, the church owes its members clear teaching about what the sacrament means and does. *Come to the Waters* (especially Part Two, section 2) offers valuable guidance for such teaching.

Baptism is not a requirement for salvation. Our salvation is a free gift of God made possible by the work of Christ. Therefore, there is really no such thing as what may be called "an emergency baptism" in United Methodism. If a newborn child, for example, dies without having been baptized, that child is received into the loving arms of God as surely as the one who has been baptized. God can and does work both through and outside of the sacraments, both through and outside of the church. But, this does not mean that baptism is unimportant or optional. John Wesley wrote of the sacrament as "...the *ordinary* means which [God] hath appointed...and to which God hath tied *us*, though he may not have tied

The claim that baptism is unrepeatable rests on the steadfast faithfulness of God. God's initiative establishes the covenant of grace into which we are incorporated in baptism. By misusing our God-given freedom, we may live in neglect or defiance of that covenant, but we cannot destroy God's love for us. When we repent and return to God, the covenant does not need to be remade, because God has always remained faithful to it. What is needed is renewal of our commitment and reaffirmation of our side of the covenant.

God's gift of grace in the baptismal covenant does not save us apart from our human response of faith. Baptized persons may have many significant spiritual experiences which they will desire to celebrate publicly in the worship life of the Church. Such experiences may include defining moments of conversion, repentance of sin, gifts of the Spirit, deepening of commitment, changes in Christian vocation, important transitions in the life of discipleship. These occasions call not for repetition of baptism, but for reaffirmations of baptismal vows as a witness to the good news that while we may be unfaithful, God is not. Appropriate services for such events would be "Confirmation or Reaffirmation of Faith" (see Baptismal Covenant I in *The United Methodist Hymnal*) or "A Celebration of New Beginnings in Faith" (*The United Methodist Book of Worship*, pages 588-90).

himself" (from the "Treatise on Baptism," 10:193). God has chosen to give us the gift of baptism as the ordinary way that people are brought into the church—the community of the new covenant. God expects us to utilize this marvelous gift in our work of shaping people as Christians. However, our failure to be faithful in our use of the sacraments does not mean that God cannot bring people to salvation through other means.

While there is no explicit statement in the New Testament that the infants of Christian families are to be baptized, there is significant evidence in that direction. Since the Jews were accustomed to including their (male) infant children in the covenant community, a radically different practice in Christianity would surely have needed some explanation. Instead, we find several passages that indicate that the children of Christian families received the sign of the new covenant community. Consider these passages with this idea in mind: Acts 2:38-41, 16:13-15, 30-33, and 1 Corinthians 1:16.

ONE BAPTISM

When baptism is understood as an act of God through which people are initiated into covenant with God and into the church—the community of the covenant—it should be obvious that baptism is not a repeatable act. While this has long been the predominant opinion in Christianity as a whole and in United Methodism in particular, there have always been some who have raised questions. It is then quite significant that the 1996 General Conference clarified our church's position by affirming that "the practice of re-baptism does not conform with God's action in baptism and is not consistent with Wesleyan tradition and the historic teaching of the church" (¶ 341.7 in *The Book of Discipline—2004*).

The essential truth is that God never fails to maintain the divine side of the covenant into which we are initiated by baptism. Therefore, that covenant can never be destroyed and never needs remaking. Human beings fail to maintain their side of the covenant. But, because God continues to be faithful, the covenant we have violated, even repudiated, still endures. What is necessary is that we repent and return to it. While no analogy is perfect, it may be helpful to consider the marriage covenant between two people. One partner may violate the covenant, even live for many years in repudiation and denial of it. But, unless a divorce has been granted, if and when that erring partner repents and returns to the relationship, the couple does not get married all over again. Indeed, they cannot "remarry" because they are still married. What is needed is the reaffirmation of the marriage covenant—recommitment to living faithfully within it. We cannot get a divorce from God, and God never divorces us. The baptismal covenant as a divine gift and promise remains in spite of our neglect or defiance of it. God's covenant endures, waiting for our return and recommitment. The baptismal covenant does not need remaking; indeed, it cannot be remade. Instead, it should be reaffirmed. (I insist upon placing the word "re-baptism" in quotation marks because in reality there is no such thing.)

To insist that the divine side of the covenant is always maintained does not mean that human actions are unimportant. Because God has given us freedom to choose, our response of faith is essential if God's offer of salvation is to be realized in our lives. (Refer to Session Two for more discussion of this point.) In spite of God's faithfulness, we can fall from faith at any point in our journey of salvation and lose our reconciled relationship with God. We will not finally be saved because we are baptized, but because we continue to accept divine grace in trusting faith.

Our faithful response to God is not a once-and-for-all event. Throughout our lives, our relationship with God will change—sometimes for the better, sometimes for the worst. Therefore, there will be numerous occasions when it is appropriate to reaffirm our baptismal vows. Such occasions will include times when we need to repent for a violation of the covenant and recommit ourselves to the covenant. Other times might be at points in our lives when we have experienced God's activity in new ways and desire to express our response. People who request "re-baptism" often do so because the church has had no other way for them to celebrate their significant spiritual experiences. If pastors and teachers will conscientiously lead their people into understanding the baptismal covenant and offer other meaningful opportunities for renewal and rededication, such requests will largely disappear. In addition to the services mentioned in the text, the "Baptismal Covenant IV" offers the entire congregation the opportunity to reaffirm their baptism.

Leader Helps

RESOURCES AND MATERIALS
- Copies of the study guide
- Bibles
- Copies of *The United Methodist Hymnal*
- Copies of *The Book of Discipline*
- Chalkboard or newsprint
- Chalk or felt-tip markers

SESSION GUIDE

1. Have the participants review the sections "Sacramental Understanding" and "Adult Baptism" (p. 27). Ask them to think about what it would be like to visit their church as an adult who had not grown up in the Christian faith. Use these questions to stimulate discussion:
   - What would be confusing for the person?
   - What would encourage the person to come again?
   - How does our church help adults who are exploring the Christian faith understand and experience what it means to be a Christian?
   - How does our church help new adult Christians grow in their faith?

2. Have the participants review the section "Infant Baptism" (p. 28) and "Baptism as God's Gift to Persons of Any Age" from *By Water and the Spirit.* Reflect on the ways your congregation currently nurtures the faith of children and youth Have the group imagine what changes might occur if the congregation took their responsibilities for the nurture of all children even more seriously.

3. Study paragraphs 4-9 of the baptismal ritual (reprinted on pp. 53-54), noting the questions about their own faith and life, and the responsibilities that are accepted by people who are bringing their infants to receive the sacrament. Compose a list of all the ways that a congregation could help parents and sponsors live out the baptismal covenant. Keep track of the ideas on newsprint or a chalkboard. Circle the things that the congregation is currently doing.

4. Have the participants review the section "One Baptism" on page 31 and the section "God's Faithfulness to the Baptismal Covenant" in *By Water and the Spirit.* Explain that some churches of other denominations are often said to practice "re-baptism" because they require people who have been baptized as infants and/or people who have been baptized by sprinkling (or pouring) to be immersed before they can be accepted as members. It is important to recognize that such a practice is not really "re-baptism," and those who require it do not understand it as such. Repetition of baptism is actually a denial of the validity of a person's previous baptism. What is being said is not that one must be baptized again, but that one has really never been baptized at all. Use this information to stimulate discussion.

5. Ask the participants to react to this statement: If baptism is an act of God through the church, any redoing of the sacrament is a statement that God failed to do what God had promised.

6. Encourage the participants to read Session Five in preparation for the next session.

TO EXPAND THIS STUDY

- In *The United Methodist Book of Worship*, pages 81-83, there is a brief, but very helpful, discussion of several of the themes within this session. Utilize it in whatever way will be most meaningful.

- Use this quote from *Remember Who You Are* by William H. Willimon to stimulate discussion of how infant baptism is an authentic presentation of the good news of salvation:

   > But wherever salvation is viewed primarily as a gift, the corporate bestowal of something that cannot be earned, merited, achieved, or bought, then babies may be baptized. The only requirement to receive a gift is to be receptive. The only requirement to be helped is to be helpless. And what is more receptive, helpless, dependent, weak, and needy than a baby?...We baptize babies not because they are better than the rest of us. The only advantage that babies have over us adults is that babies may be less confused than we about the limits of their ability to save themselves. Is that why Jesus said that the Kingdom belongs to them? (p. 65)

- Another quotation from Dr. Willimon should serve to open a discussion of God's faithfulness:

   > I do not always feel like a child of God. I do not always look like a child of God. God knows I do not always act like a child of God! But I am. I am one of God's children not because of what I did or because of who I am but because God chose me....I am owned (*Remember Who You Are*, p. 41).

Nurturing People in the Life of Faith

Nurturing Persons in the Life of Faith

If persons are to be enabled to live faithfully the human side of the baptismal covenant, Christian nurture is essential. Christian nurture builds on baptism and is itself a means of grace. For infant baptism, an early step is instruction prior to baptism of parent(s) or sponsors in the Gospel message, the meaning of the sacrament, and the responsibilities of a Christian home. The pastor has specific responsibility for this step (*The Book of Discipline*, par. 439.1.b.). Adults who are candidates for baptism need careful preparation for receiving this gift of grace and living out its meaning (*The Book of Discipline*, par. 216.1.).

After baptism, the faithful Church provides the nurture which makes possible a comprehensive and lifelong process of growing in grace. The content of this nurturing will be appropriate to the stages of life and maturity of faith of individuals. Christian nurture includes both cognitive learning and spiritual formation. A crucial goal is the bringing of persons to recognition of their need for salvation and their acceptance of God's gift in Jesus Christ. Those experiencing conversion and commitment to Christ are to profess their faith in a public ritual. They will need to be guided and supported

BEGINNING THE JOURNEY

We have stressed repeatedly throughout these sessions that the journey of salvation is lifelong, a journey in which we are shaped ever more fully into the image of Christ. This is not a journey that an individual undertakes alone. During every step of the way, we need careful and continual nurture by other people in the Christian community.

Ideally, this process should begin even prior to the birth of a child. While parents are preparing for the experience of childbirth and planning for the care of the newborn, they can also be learning about their privileges and responsibilities as Christian parents. Practically speaking, expectant parents have much more time to attend classes, read, study, and pray than they will after their child's birth. This may be the best opportunity the church has to teach parents about the significance of infant baptism and how to begin the joyous task of bringing up their child in the Christian faith. Pastors and teachers who work with parents not only need to help them understand the vows and promises that they will take in the baptism of their baby, but also guide them in planning how they will actually carry out their pledges.

NURTURE: HOME AND CHURCH

As baptized children grow up, they need constant and intentional nurture. This nurture should include both instruction and demonstration. Children need not only to hear, but also to see what it means to be Christian. The two chief places where Christians can be formed are in the home and in the church. In the secular, even pagan, culture in which we currently live, no other agency of society can be relied upon for the religious training of our children. Indeed, both home and church are challenged to diligent efforts to counteract the many negative influences to which children are inevitably exposed. Christian nurture in the home might include prayer and Bible reading; honest discussion of religious and moral questions; faithful stewardship of financial resources and time; actions of charity and social justice; attitudes of respect for all people as equally loved and valued by God; employment of abilities in meaningful labor; choices of wholesome recreation and leisure-time activities; and, perhaps of greatest importance, the life examples that model Christlike love.

throughout their lives of discipleship. Through its worship life, its Christian education programs, its spiritual growth emphases, its social action and mission, its examples of Christian discipleship, and its offering of the various means of grace, the Church strives to shape persons into the image of Christ. Such nurturing enables Christians to live out the transforming potential of the grace of their baptism.

Profession of Christian Faith and Confirmation

The Christian life is a dynamic process of change and growth, marked at various points by celebrations in rituals of the saving grace of Christ. The Holy Spirit works in the lives of persons prior to their baptism, is at work in their baptism, and continues to work in their lives after their baptism. When persons recognize and accept this activity of the Holy Spirit, they respond with renewed faith and commitment.

In the early Church, baptism, the laying on of hands, and eucharist were a unified rite of initiation and new birth for Christians of all ages. During the Middle Ages in Western Europe, confirmation was separated from baptism in both time and theology. A misunderstanding developed of confirmation as completing baptism, with emphasis upon human vows and initiation into church membership. John Wesley did not recommend confirmation to his preachers or to the new Methodist church in America. Since 1964 in the former Methodist Church, the first public profession of faith for those baptized as infants has been called Confirmation. In the former Evangelical United Brethren Church,

Parents can be greatly aided in these endeavors by members of the extended family, by friends, and other exemplary individuals. Especially in a time when so many children live in single-parent households and in shifting family situations, it is doubly important for parents to have the assistance of other adults. Parents should seriously consider asking other Christians to serve as sponsors for their child. Such sponsors might participate in the baptismal service and function as counselors and mentors as the child grows up. (See paragraph 7 in the "Baptismal Covenant I.")

The privilege and responsibility of nurturing children in the Christian faith do not belong only to the parents and other adults who have already been mentioned. Neither, of course, is the home the only place where such nurture needs to take place. As the community of faith, the entire congregation shares in the joy and the task. Church members are not spectators when a new member is being baptized into the body of Christ; they are participants. (See paragraphs 8, 9, and 16 in the "Baptismal Covenant I.") Every baptismal occasion should be a means of grace for all people present as they reaffirm their own baptism and commit themselves to nurture the new members.

The church itself is a means of grace in the lives of children who are growing up within it—an instrument for the shaping of Christians. The church does this in a variety of ways, formal and informal. These include public worship, Sunday school, vacation Bible school, United Methodist Youth Fellowship, choirs and other musical groups, camping, service projects, and mission trips. Perhaps of equal importance is the personal influence of pastors, teachers, counselors, and other caring adults who not only instruct and educate, but also listen and inspire. Christian nurture should include both the cognitive process of learning and the spiritual process of formation.

CONFIRMATION

The fruits of the process of nurture find public expression in the individual's first affirmation of the baptismal covenant— what we now call confirmation. Traditionally in early adolescence, young people are offered a special series of programs designed to inform them about the church and the faith, as well as to promote their spiritual formation. These programs, commonly called "confirmation classes," are done in a variety of ways in United Methodism. Unfortunately, the effectiveness of some of them is called into question by statistics showing that many young people—and their families—regard confirmation as "graduation from the church." Focused preparation for confirmation is very valuable, but it must be understood as one step in a process of nurture and decision-making that will continue throughout a person's life.

there was no such rite until union with The Methodist Church in 1968. With the restoration of confirmation—as the laying on of hands—to the current baptismal ritual, it should be emphasized that confirmation is what the Holy Spirit does. Confirmation is a divine action, the work of the Spirit empowering a person "born through water and the Spirit" to "live as a faithful disciple of Jesus Christ."

An adult or youth preparing for baptism should be carefully instructed in its life-transforming significance and responsibilities. Such a person professes in the sacrament of baptism his or her faith in Jesus Christ and commitment to discipleship, is offered the gift of assurance, and is confirmed by the power of the Holy Spirit (see Baptismal Covenant I, sections 4, 11, and 12). No separate ritual of confirmation is needed for the believing person.

An infant who is baptized cannot make a personal profession of faith as a part of the sacrament. Therefore, as the young person is nurtured and matures so as to be able to respond to God's grace, conscious faith and intentional commitment are necessary. Such a person must come to claim the faith of the Church proclaimed in baptism as her or his own faith. Deliberate preparation for this event focuses on the young person's self-understanding and appropriation of Christian doctrines, spiritual disciplines, and life of discipleship. It is a special time for experiencing divine grace and for consciously embracing one's Christian vocation as a part of the priesthood of all believers. Youth who were not baptized as infants share in the same period of preparation for profession of Christian

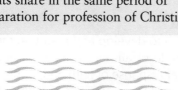

One of the great strengths of our current baptismal ritual is that it makes very clear that an individual becomes a member of the church through baptism. Baptism is an initiation into the church, an incorporation into the body of Christ. This clarity about the meaning of baptism, however, has left confusion about the meaning of what the church has called confirmation. Perhaps a brief look at the understandings of confirmation in the history of the church might help us.

In the early centuries of Christianity, confirmation was a part of the service of baptism. It followed the administration of the water, and it included the laying on of hands by the priest with anointing and the sign of the cross. These ritual acts were used regardless of the age of the person being baptized. In the part of Christianity that developed into the Eastern Orthodox Church, this ritual continued to be used within one service of initiation, which also included the first communion. This is the practice of those churches today. In the western part of the church—western Europe and Africa—that developed into the Roman Catholic Church, the unified ritual became divided into separate services occurring at different times. This happened largely because it was believed that only a bishop could confirm. Because a bishop was not always available at every baptism, practical necessity resulted in confirmation being practiced as a separate rite.

Over the centuries, confirmation came to be regarded in the Roman Catholic Church as a separate sacrament. It is understood as a work of the Holy Spirit, bestowing divine grace to strengthen an individual for the new opportunities and temptations of life as an adult. The Protestant churches, which developed out of the Reformation in the sixteenth century, rejected the idea of confirmation as a sacrament. These Calvinist, Lutheran, and Anglican traditions instead emphasized the necessity of catechesis, or teaching of the faith, to those who had been baptized as infants. Confirmation became understood as a ceremony in which those who had learned the catechism and other basics of the faith publicly professed their Christian commitment. Participation in confirmation was usually required before a young person could receive Holy Communion.

When John Wesley revised the Anglican *Book of Common Prayer* to serve as a worship book for North American Methodists, he omitted confirmation completely. Wesley recognized baptism as the sacrament of Christian initiation and required no other ceremony between baptism and Holy Communion. Although he provided no ritual for their celebration, Wesley did emphasize the necessity of conversion, spiritual rebirth, and personal faith in Christ. American Methodism con-

faith. For them, it is nurture for baptism, for becoming members of the Church, and for confirmation.

When persons who were baptized as infants are ready to profess their Christian faith, they participate in the service which United Methodism now calls Confirmation. This occasion is not an entrance into Church membership, for this was accomplished through baptism. It is the first public affirmation of the grace of God in one's baptism and the acknowledgment of one's acceptance of that grace by faith. This moment includes all the elements of conversion—repentance of sin, surrender and death of self, trust in the saving grace of God, new life in Christ, and becoming an instrument of God's purpose in the world. The profession of Christian faith, to be celebrated in the midst of the worshiping congregation, should include the voicing of baptismal vows as a witness to faith and the opportunity to give testimony to personal Christian experience.

Confirmation follows profession of the Christian faith as part of the same service. Confirmation is a dynamic action of the Holy Spirit that can be repeated. In confirmation the outpouring of the Holy Spirit is invoked to provide the one being confirmed with the power to live in the faith that he or she has professed. The basic meaning of confirmation is strengthening and making firm in Christian faith and life. The ritual action in confirmation is the laying on of hands as the sign of God's continuing gift of the grace of Pentecost. Historically, the person being confirmed was also anointed on the forehead with oil in the shape of a cross as a mark of the Spirit's work.

tinued this evangelical emphasis but had no rituals for receiving people into church membership until the time of the Civil War. The term "confirmation" does not appear in Methodist rituals until the 1964 *Hymnal*. Because of its recent adoption and the diversity of its meaning in other churches, United Methodism continues to have some difficulties, both with the name and the practice. Confirmation has generally been understood as an expression of conversion and a service of "joining the church." This may be confusing since our current ritual makes it clear that an individual becomes a member of the church at baptism.

Our current Services of the Baptismal Covenant reunify the various parts into which Christian initiation had been divided. These services for people of any age combine baptism with water and the Spirit, the laying on of hands with anointing and the sign of the cross, and first Communion. (See paragraph 11 and 12 in the "Baptismal Covenant I.") When youth or adults are baptized, they profess faith in Christ in the vows of the ritual. They come to baptism in repentance and faith, and are mature enough to affirm their Christian commitment at the time of their baptism. Infants who are baptized will make their own public profession of faith some years later. Their repentance and faith will be professed when they have been appropriately nurtured and are sufficiently mature to be able to make their Christian commitment. What United Methodism means by confirmation is chiefly the public profession of faith that follows Christian teaching and conversion. This profession is the individual's first public affirmation of the baptismal covenant. It is the profession of a commitment to Christ as Lord and Savior, an acceptance of the privileges and responsibilities of membership in the church, and the intention, in the words of the ritual, "to live as a faithful disciple of Jesus Christ."

While the individual Christian is confirming his or her own faith, the greater act of confirmation is that of the Holy Spirit, who blesses the person with strengthened faith for living out the Christian calling. This work of the Spirit is expressed in the words of the pastor and the act of laying on of hands by the pastor and others, symbolic of the presence and power of the Spirit. Another ancient symbolic action may also be used—anointing with oil in the sign of the cross.

REAFFIRMING OUR BAPTISM

It is essential for the church to develop and maintain the various means by which people of all ages are taught and nurtured toward their personal response of faith and commitment to Christ. In confirmation and the profession of faith, whether they are part of the sacrament of baptism or on a later occasion, individuals make their first public affirmation of commit-

The ritual of the baptismal covenant included in *The United Methodist Hymnal* makes clear that the first and primary confirming act of the Holy Spirit is in connection with and immediately follows baptism.

When a baptized person has professed her or his Christian faith and been confirmed, that person enters more fully into the responsibilities and privileges of membership in the Church. Just as infants are members of their human families, but unable to participate in all aspects of family life, so baptized infants are members of the Church—the family of faith—but not yet capable of sharing in all that membership involves. For this reason, statistics of church membership are counts of professed/confirmed members rather than of all baptized members.

Reaffirmation of One's Profession of Christian Faith

The life of faith which baptized persons live is like a pilgrimage or journey. On this lifelong journey there are many challenges, changes, and chances. We engage life's experiences on our journey of faith as a part of the redeeming and sanctifying Body of Christ. Ongoing Christian nurture teaches, shapes, and strengthens us to live ever more faithfully as we are open to the Spirit's revealing more and more of the way and will of God. As our appreciation of the good news of Jesus Christ deepens and our commitment to Christ's service becomes more profound, we seek occasions to celebrate. Like God's people through the ages, all Christians need to participate in acts of renewal within the covenant community. Such an opportunity is

ment to the baptismal covenant. But, it must always be remembered that salvation is not just an event, but a journey. The process of growing in grace and holiness never ends. The church clearly needs to teach and nurture individuals toward an initial profession of faith and an ongoing plan for Christian formation. This is, indeed, the task of the church—to form people into authentic Christians. During a life of Christian discipleship, there will be other occasions when it is appropriate to reaffirm one's commitment to the baptismal covenant. (See paragraph 2 of the "Baptismal Covenant I.") Some of these occasions will be shared with other members of the congregation. Each time that the sacrament of baptism is celebrated, it is a time for every Christian present to reaffirm her or his own baptismal vows. In paragraph 8 of the "Baptismal Covenant I," the congregation is explicitly asked to "reaffirm both your rejection of sin and your commitment to Christ." This is followed by a congregational pledge to accept the responsibility of nurturing other Christians. In paragraph 9, the congregation joins with those being baptized and/or confirmed in a declaration of faith using the Apostles' Creed.

The covenant community of God's people in the Old Testament came together regularly to celebrate God's faithfulness and to reaffirm their own commitment. Our current ritual includes a new service that provides a powerful opportunity for us to join with other Christians in this kind of reaffirmation. The "Baptismal Covenant IV" may be used on any occasion of corporate worship. It is particularly appropriate for celebration of special days in the life of the church, such as Easter, Pentecost, All Saints Day, and the Baptism of Christ. Other meaningful times might be at the close of a retreat; at annual, district, or charge conference sessions; at annual conference, district, or local meetings of United Methodist Women, Men, or Youth Fellowship; at the end of a study of baptism. Water should be used in this service as a reminder of its rich significance in the story of salvation. People might come to the font and look at the water, touch it, perhaps trace with water the sign of the cross on their foreheads. The pastor might sign each worshiper with water as he or she says, "Remember your baptism and be thankful." It is important that water be used in ways that are clearly a remembrance, rather than a repetition of baptism.

In addition to these corporate celebrations, our rituals provide opportunities for public acts of renewal by individuals. This can be done by using portions of the baptismal ritual for reaffirmation. Another meaningful service for such occasions is "A Celebration of New Beginnings in Faith" from *The Book of Worship*. These services meet the needs of individuals who in the past might have asked for "re-baptism." (*Come to the*

offered in every occasion of baptism when the congregation remembers and affirms the gracious work of God which baptism celebrates. Baptismal Covenant IV in *The United Methodist Hymnal* is a powerful ritual of reaffirmation which uses water in ways which remind us of our baptism. The historic "Covenant Renewal Service" and "Love Feast" can also be used for this purpose (*The United Methodist Book of Worship*, pages 288-94 and 581-84). Reaffirmation of faith is a human response to God's grace and therefore may be repeated at many points in our faith journey.

Waters, Part Two, section 3 will be useful here.) They can be used when people have experienced deeper conversion, growth in holiness, gifts of the Spirit, repentance and restoration, new calls to service, changed life circumstances, strengthened faith. Pastors should encourage church members to utilize these celebrations of the ongoing grace of baptism working throughout life.

The words "Remember your baptism and be thankful" do not refer to a recollection of a specific event in life. Obviously, one who was baptized as an infant cannot recall that occasion to conscious memory. What is being remembered and celebrated is the gift of divine grace, which is not a one-time occurrence, but rather a continuing reality. There are, however, ways to help people, especially children, more meaningfully "remember" their baptism. The baptismal service might be audiotaped or videotaped or recorded in photographs. (Obviously this needs to be done in a way that is not distracting.) The church should give baptismal certificates and, perhaps, items (a candle, for example) used in the service. All of these things can then be used by parents as they teach their growing children about what it means to be baptized. Family observances of baptismal anniversaries can make the celebrations of spiritual birth as joyous as those of physical birthdays. Surely the church should recognize baptismal anniversaries by listing the anniversary dates and the names of the baptized in monthly church newsletters. The possibilities are endless, if we only make a creative effort. One of my students told me recently that she had written a long letter to her infant son on the day of his baptism. Imagine what this could mean later on in that child's life.

In all of our reaffirmations of baptism, we are reminding ourselves of our identity as a people called by God, gifted with divine grace, and living in the continuing presence of God's Spirit.

Leader Helps

RESOURCES AND MATERIALS
- Copies of the study guide
- Bibles
- Copies of *The United Methodist Hymnal*
- Chalkboard or newsprint
- Chalk or felt-tip markers

SESSION GUIDE

1. Tertullian, a Christian leader in the third century, wrote that, "Christians are made, not born." Write this quotation on the board and use it to stimulate discussion about the necessity of Christian nurture. Note also Jesus' instructions to make disciples, baptizing and teaching (Matthew 28:18-20).

2. Have the participants review the section "Beginning the Journey" on page 35 and paragraph 5 of the "Baptismal Covenant I" (p. 53) in which parents pledge to nurture their baptized children in the Christian faith. If there are parents in the class, ask them to remember what they did to prepare spiritually for the birth or adoption of their children. Identify ways that your congregation does and could help expectant parents prepare for Christian parenthood. (If there are specific suggestions for things the congregation could do that they are not currently doing, help the participants identify the steps that would need to occur to make these things a reality in the congregation.)

3. Have the participants review the section "Nurture: Home and Church" on page 35. Examine the congregation's plan for the process of shaping Christians. Help the participants identify how both the cognitive process of learning and the spiritual process of formation are included in the plan. Some congregations may discover they are emphasizing one of these two aspects and may need to explore ways they can be more balanced in their approach to nurturing young Christians.

4. Have the group examine paragraphs 11, 12, 14, and 15 of the "Baptismal Covenant I" (p. 55). Note particularly what is being done by God and what is

being asked of the person being baptized and/or confirmed. Observe the difference in the tenses of the verbs in the words of the pastor in paragraphs 11 and 12. In paragraph 11 (used at the baptismal service), the phrase "being born through water and the Spirit" implies that this spiritual birth is presently happening. In paragraph 12 (used in the confirmation service), the phrase "having been born through water and the Spirit" indicates that this birth has already happened; the covenant offered by God has been accepted.

5. Review the section "Confirmation" beginning on page 36 and the section "Profession of Christian Faith and Confirmation" from *By Water and the Spirit*. Discuss what the following quote by John Gooch, editor of the United Methodist confirmation resources, says not only about the appropriate age for confirmation, but also about the meaning of it:

> ...if we see confirmation as somehow providing for a person all that he or she will ever need for faith and life, then confirmation should probably be postponed as long as possible. But if we see confirmation as one step in a lifelong process of nurture and decision, then the age for confirmation is not nearly as important. If we see confirmation as a repeatable rite, one that affirms growth in faith at any age, then the age question is almost irrelevant, because we will be doing confirmation with individuals at different points all their lives (*Circuit Rider*, March 1995, pp. 12-13).

6. Review the section "Reaffirming Our Baptism" beginning on page 39 and the section "Reaffirmation of One's Profession of Christian Faith" from *By Water and the Spirit*. Have the participants add their own ideas to the suggestions given for helping people "remember" their baptism in ways that make baptismal grace a conscious reality in their lives.

7. Begin planning to celebrate a service of Reaffirmation of the Baptismal Covenant at the conclusion of this series of studies.

8. Encourage the participants to read Session Six in preparation for the next session.

To Expand This Study

- Part Two, section 2 in *Come to the Waters* by Daniel Benedict offers much helpful material as the church seeks to strengthen its work of Christian nurture. Use as much of this as time allows to help the group recognize some possibilities for your congregation. Perhaps a few people could volunteer to study this resource in more detail and report to the group later.

- Consider together the account in Joshua 24 of a ceremony of covenant renewal. Discuss why we as human beings constantly need to renew our covenants.

- *The Book of Worship* contains rich resources for use in both corporate and individual reaffirmations of baptismal faith. Look at the "Covenant Renewal Service" (p. 288), the "Love Feast" (p. 581), and the "New Beginnings in Faith" (p. 588). Discuss how these services might be used in your church.

- Look in the *Hymnal* at the "Baptismal Covenant IV: Congregational Reaffirmation of the Baptismal Covenant." Note its similarity to the service of baptism itself. Discuss how this service is being, or could be, used in the life of your congregation.

Baptism in Relation to Other Rites of the Church

Baptism in Relation to Other Rites of the Church

The grace of God which claims us in our baptism is made available to us in many other ways and, especially, through other rites of the Church.

Baptism and the Lord's Supper (Holy Communion or Eucharist)

Through baptism, persons are initiated into the Church; by the Lord's Supper, the Church is sustained in the life of faith. The Services of the Baptismal Covenant appropriately conclude with Holy Communion, through which the union of the new member with the Body of Christ is most fully expressed. Holy Communion is a sacred meal in which the community of faith, in the simple act of eating bread and drinking wine, proclaims and participates in all that God has done, is doing, and will continue to do for us in Christ. In celebrating the Eucharist, we remember the grace given to us in our baptism and partake of the spiritual food necessary for sustaining and fulfilling the promises of salvation. Because the table at which we gather belongs to the Lord, it should be open to all who respond to Christ's love, regardless of age or church membership. The Wesleyan tradition has always recognized that Holy Communion may be an occasion for the reception of converting, justifying,

HOLY COMMUNION

Throughout these sessions we have repeatedly emphasized that God's grace is given to God's people in and through baptism. But we have tried to make clear, especially in Session Two, that in the United Methodist tradition there are a variety of means through which God's grace comes to us. Among these are other significant ritual celebrations in the church that we want to consider in this last session—Holy Communion, Christian ministry, marriage, and death and resurrection. It is important to recognize that these services are closely related to, even grounded upon, baptism.

The names "the Lord's Supper," "Holy Communion," and "Eucharist" all refer to the same service, but emphasize different aspects of it. To speak of the Lord's Supper is to be reminded of Jesus' last meal with the Twelve and that he instructed his disciples, then and now, to continue to partake together of the bread and wine in remembrance of his ministry and death on that occasion. To speak of Holy Communion is to emphasize that we share this meal with other people and with Christ. We are not a collection of individuals. We are a community bound together as the body of Christ. The word "Eucharist" means thanksgiving. In using it we are speaking of a joyous celebration of the work of Christ, which has made our salvation possible.

Holy Communion is a sacrament. Through our participation in it, we receive divine grace, which sustains us in our ongoing process of salvation. The grace that comes to us in the sacrament comes to meet our particular needs. It may be convicting or converting or justifying or sanctifying. It provides us with "bread for the journey." For this reason, John Wesley urged the early Methodists to take communion as often as they possibly could. Unfortunately, in America the scarcity of ordained ministers meant that the sacraments were not always administered regularly. Many churches got into the habit of having Holy Communion only once a quarter. Now that ordained pastors are widely available, United Methodism is slowly moving toward patterns of more frequent communion—monthly in some churches, weekly in others.

and sanctifying grace. Unbaptized persons who receive communion should be counseled and nurtured toward baptism as soon as possible.

Baptism and Christian Ministry

Through baptism, God calls and commissions persons to the general ministry of all Christian believers (see *The Book of Discipline*, 1992, par. 101-7). This ministry, in which we participate both individually and corporately, is the activity of discipleship. It is grounded upon the awareness that we have been called into a new relationship not only with God, but also with the world. The task of Christians is to embody the Gospel and the Church in the world. We exercise our calling as Christians by prayer, by witnessing to the good news of salvation in Christ, by caring for and serving other people, and by working toward reconciliation, justice, and peace in the world. This is the universal priesthood of all believers.

From within this general ministry of all believers, God calls and the Church authorizes some persons for the task of representative ministry (see *The Book of Discipline*, 1992, par. 108-10). The vocation of those in representative ministry includes focusing, modeling, supervising, shepherding, enabling, and empowering the general ministry of the Church. Their ordination to Word, Sacrament, and Order or consecration to diaconal ministries of service, justice, and love is grounded in the same baptism that commissions the general priesthood of all believers.

Holy Communion is the "family meal" of the community of faith. The community is comprised of those initiated through baptism. The instructions at the end of each of the baptismal services are, "It is most fitting that the service continue with Holy Communion, in which the union of the new members with the body of Christ is most fully expressed." Note that this instruction is in the ritual for baptism of infants as well; God's family includes people of all ages. Sometimes we hear complaints that small children cannot understand what is happening in the sacrament and should not be allowed to participate. But quite honestly, can any of us truly claim to understand the mystery of God's gracious love revealed in the life, death, and resurrection of Christ? Probably the very first way that a child experiences love is through receiving food for physical hunger. Children may well grasp the intimate connection between eating/drinking and love better than we adults. Another word for sacrament is "mystery"; none of us can fully comprehend how and why God so works. Holy Communion is a gift of divine love for which we cannot be worthy. Jesus ate with sinners during his earthly ministry; in Communion the resurrected Christ meets us in all our failure and sin, and invites us to dine with him.

Just as we entertain guests at our own family meals, so Christian hospitality welcomes others to our meal with Christ. United Methodism has always insisted upon an "open table." We remember Wesley's assertion that God brings people to conversion through Holy Communion. Therefore, we acknowledge that the Table is not ours, but Christ's. If there are unbaptized people in our congregations who regularly participate in Holy Communion, it is appropriate for pastors to talk with these people to find out why they are not choosing to be initiated into the church. It may be that there is confusion or misunderstanding about baptism that the pastor can address.

CALLED TO MINISTRY

Baptism is our ordination into the general ministry of the church. All baptized Christians share this ministry; all forms of service to the church and to the world have their foundation here. *The Book of Discipline—2004* expresses this idea very well: "... all Christians are called to minister wherever Christ would have them serve and witness in deeds and words that heal and free.... This ministry of all Christians in Christ's name and spirit is both a gift and a task. The gift is God's unmerited grace; the task is unstinting service" (¶ ¶ 126-127). Christian laypeople do not always think of themselves as ministers of the gospel of Jesus Christ, but this is the role to which God has called them and to which baptism has commissioned them. The second vow in the baptismal ritual—"Do you accept the freedom and power God gives you to resist evil, injustice, and

Baptism and Christian Marriage

In the ritual for marriage, the minister addresses the couple: "I ask you now, in the presence of God and these people, to declare your intention to enter into union with one another through the grace of Jesus Christ, who calls you into union with himself as acknowledged in your baptism" (*The United Methodist Hymnal*, page 865). Marriage is to be understood as a covenant of love and commitment with mutual promises and responsibilities. For the Church, the marriage covenant is grounded in the covenant between God and God's people into which Christians enter in their baptism. The love and fidelity which are to characterize Christian marriage will be a witness to the gospel and the couple are to "Go to serve God and your neighbor in all that you do."

When ministers officiate at the marriage of a couple who are not both Christians, the ritual needs to be altered to protect the integrity of all involved.

Baptism and Christian Funeral

The Christian Gospel is a message of death and resurrection, that of Christ and our own. Baptism signifies our dying and rising with Christ. As death no longer has dominion over Christ, we believe that if we have died with Christ we shall also live with him (Romans 6:8-9). As the liturgy of the Service of Death and Resurrection proclaims: "Dying, Christ destroyed our death. Rising, Christ restored our life. Christ will come again in glory. As in baptism (Name) put on Christ, so in

oppression in whatever forms they present themselves?"—is a call to ministry. The general ministry of all Christians is powerfully described in ¶ ¶ 220–221 of *The Book of Discipline*.

"The priesthood of all believers" means not only that each of us has access to God in Christ, but also that each of us is to function as a priest to other people. We are to be instruments through which God can work, channels of divine love into places of deep need. Too often we tend to define ourselves by our secular occupations, to think of ourselves as primarily teachers, farmers, or salespeople. In our baptism, God tells us that we are primarily ministers; ministry is our highest calling and heaviest responsibility. What a difference Christians could make in the world if we accepted and fulfilled this role! The ministry of most may not occur chiefly in or through the church. As laypeople we can reach and touch people who would never come to the church—co-workers, acquaintances, and friends. Our ministry of daily life can be the most fruitful service for Christ that most people will ever experience.

Those who are commonly referred to as ordained ministers are set apart by the church in response to God's call on their lives. They serve in the ministry of representing Christ to the church and the church to the world. Like the call of the laity to ministry, the call of the clergy is grounded in their identity and commitment as baptized disciples of Christ. The 1996 General Conference altered the forms of clergy leadership. The United Methodist Church now has two groups of clergy—deacons who are ordained to ministries of Word and Service, and elders who are ordained to Service, Word, Sacrament, and Order. Some of those who are currently serving in diaconal ministry, a ministry of consecrated laypeople, will seek ordination as deacons; others will choose to remain as diaconal ministers. Since January 1, 1997, there have been no new candidates accepted for diaconal ministry.

In a deeper sense, ordained clergy share with laity the responsibilities and the privileges of a ministry that represent Christ to the world. All authentic expressions of ministry are those manifested in the "living out" of our baptism.

MARRIAGE

Our current ritual understands the marriage of Christians as a part of both partners living out the identity and calling that they received in baptism. Marriage is a covenant relationship, and its fulfillment depends on the prior covenant between God and God's people. In the Old and New Testaments, the relationships between God and Israel and between God and the church are portrayed by using the metaphor of marriage. Of course, unlike covenants with God, the marriage covenant

Christ may (Name) be clothed with Glory" (*The United Methodist Hymnal*, page 870).

If the deceased person was never baptized, the ritual needs to be amended in ways which continue to affirm the truths of the Gospel, but are appropriate to the situation.

Committal of the deceased to God and the body to its final resting place recall the act of baptism and derive Christian meaning from God's baptismal covenant with us. We acknowledge the reality of death and the pain of loss, and we give thanks for the life that was lived and shared with us. We worship in the awareness that our gathering includes the whole communion of saints, visible and invisible, and that in Christ the ties of love unite the living and the dead.

Conclusion

Baptism is a crucial threshold that we cross on our journey in faith. But there are many others, including the final transition from death to life eternal. Through baptism we are incorporated into the ongoing history of Christ's mission and we are identified and made participants in God's new history in Jesus Christ and the new age that Christ is bringing. We await the final moment of grace, when Christ comes in victory at the end of the age to bring all who are in Christ into the glory of that victory. Baptism has significance in time and gives meaning to the end of time. In it we have a vision of a world recreated and humanity transformed and exalted by God's presence. We are told that in this new heaven and new earth there will be no

is between two people who are equal. Human relationships characterized by self-giving love are expressions of divine love. Rich and challenging opportunities for ministry will be found in the marriage and family life. Christian marriage is to be a place in which people experience and express the sanctifying grace of God as they grow in holiness of life. Strengthened by the grace received in their relationship, each partner will be able to serve more effectively those inside and outside his or her home.

Contrary to past practice when it appeared only in sources used by pastors, the ritual for marriage is printed in the current *Hymnal*. This is because the service is to be an occasion of corporate worship in which the congregation participates. The marriage of Christians is not a private event, but one that involves the community of faith into which the couple was incorporated by baptism.

There are some situations when pastors may find it necessary to decline an invitation to officiate at a wedding. The only kind of marriage that the church offers is Christian marriage. If that is not what a couple wants or are able to commit to, they should be counseled to have a civil ceremony. In some other cases, only one of the partners may be a Christian. Pastors will then need to adapt the wording of the service so that no one is asked to speak falsely.

DEATH AND RESURRECTION

The call to Christian discipleship is a call to come and die. In living out our baptism, we fulfill that call. Christ's claim upon our lives means that, if we are faithful, we are constantly dying to the things that compete for our loyalty. Jesus spoke of the necessity of taking up the cross—an instrument of execution—not once, but continually. Christians should be good at dying; we have practiced for it in the daily sacrifices and surrenders that the life of love demands. Christians are also very good at living; we are in a loving relationship with the One who not only gives life eternal, but also fills life with meaning and joy.

Images of death and resurrection are among the most common ways of understanding baptism. Baptism is the death of the old sinful self and the birth of a new spiritual life in Christ. We can also turn this idea around and use baptism as a way of understanding death and resurrection. In our baptism what appeared to be only death was really a birth; thus, physical death is actually the beginning of a new kind of existence. Death and resurrection bring the fulfillment of the spiritual life into which we were born through our baptism. Christian

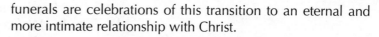

temple, for even our churches and services of worship will have had their time and ceased to be, in the presence of God, "the first and the last, the beginning and the end" (Revelation 21-22).

Until that day, we are charged by Christ to "Go therefore and make disciples of all nations, baptizing them in the name of the Father, the Son, and the Holy Spirit, and teaching them to obey everything that I have commanded you. And remember, I am with you always, to the end of the age" (Matthew 28:19-20). Baptism is at the heart of the Gospel of grace and at the core of the Church's mission. When we baptize we say what we understand as Christians about ourselves and our community: that we are loved into being by God, lost because of sin, but redeemed and saved in Jesus Christ to live new lives in anticipation of his coming again in glory. Baptism is an expression of God's love for the world, and the effects of baptism also express God's grace. As baptized people of God, we therefore respond with praise and thanksgiving, praying that God's will be done in our own lives:

"We your people stand before you,
water-washed and Spirit-born.
By your grace, our lives we offer,
Recreate us; God, transform!"

Ruth Duck,
"Wash, O God, Our Sons and Daughters"
(*The United Methodist Hymnal*, 605)
Used with permission.

funerals are celebrations of this transition to an eternal and more intimate relationship with Christ.

The "Service of Death and Resurrection" is printed in the *Hymnal* and includes participation by the congregation. Funerals, burials, and memorial services are occasions of public worship for the community of faith. They are not only rites of mourning and farewell, but also services of deep joy as those gathered are reminded that there is everlasting life in Christ. Christians live, die, and are resurrected in the community of faith. The ideas of the communion of the saints (as affirmed in the creed) and the church triumphant (as sung about in hymns) perhaps become clearer to us during occasions of death.

Pastors will sometimes be called upon to lead a service for a person who was not baptized. When this is the case, some portions of the ritual will need to be omitted and others reworded. Even such difficult services must include a clear proclamation of the new life available through the risen Christ.

So What?

I often tell my students that they should ask themselves, "So what?" at the end of each sermon and lesson. This is the question that we need to focus on as our study of baptism comes to conclusion. "So what difference does any of this make to me? as an individual? as a church member?" Does anything read, said, or done in these study sessions really matter? My hope is that at the very least this study may cause you to think more seriously about what it means to be a baptized person trying to live a life of Christian discipleship in your particular time and place. My intent is that you may realize more fully the mission of the church and your own role in carrying out that mission.

Susanne Johnson writes, "What ails the church in the first instance is not that we are not 'spiritual' enough. Starkly put, we are not Christian enough! I mean that we have not taken seriously the radical, countercultural, protracted process of Christian initiation" (*Christian Spiritual Formation in the Church and Classroom*, p. 27). Baptism is initiating people into the Christian faith and church. It is a process that transcends any specific event. It is a protracted process—one that involves much time for change and growth. It is a radical and countercultural process that shapes people into Christians in defiance of the values and pressures of secular society. If we are to become "Christian enough" to share in the divine mission for the world, we must take our baptism with utter seriousness. As God's baptized people, who are we and what are we to do? Baptism tells us who God is and who God intends for us to be. We are loved more deeply by God than we can ever comprehend. God is unwilling to allow us to be less than we were created to be. We are in covenant with God; we belong to God. Baptism shows us what we are to do. We are to be God's ministers, sent by God to serve the world, to work for reconciliation, justice, and peace. Baptism makes us a part of the community of the church, charged with the responsibility of continuing the work of Christ. Baptism tells us who we are and what we are to do.

Baptism prompts self-questioning. What kind of a person are you? Are you the person you want to be? How are you growing in Christ's likeness? What are you doing with your life? How much of Christ do other people see in you? Are you helping others to know who they are in God's eyes? What gifts have you been given that you can share with those in need? What gives your life meaning? What gives your life joy? What is the purpose of the church? How is your church forming Christians? Is your congregation doing the work of Christ? What is the work of Christ in your local community, in your nation, in the world? What wrongs are the community of faith called to make right? How can the church change conditions of injustice, oppression, and poverty?

To be baptized is to have one's whole life claimed and used by God. To be a member of the church is to be a part of God's community, which is chosen and charged to carry out God's mission. Baptism finds its fulfillment in ministry. God's people must remember their baptism and be not only thankful, but fruitful.

> "The Holy Spirit work within you,
> that having been born through water and the Spirit,
> you may live as faithful disciples of Jesus Christ."

Leader Helps

RESOURCES AND MATERIALS
- Copies of the study guide
- Bibles
- Copies of *The United Methodist Hymnal*
- Chalkboard or newsprint
- Chalk or felt-tip markers

SESSION GUIDE

1. Review the section "Holy Communion" beginning on page 43 and the section "Baptism and the Lord's Supper" from *By Water and the Spirit*. Encourage discussion about both the meaning and practice of Holy Communion. Ask the participants to recall a particularly memorable communion service. Have them identify the things that made it memorable. List the things mentioned on newsprint or a chalkboard.

2. Look at "A Service of Word and Table I" found on page 6 of the *Hymnal*. If possible use a worship bulletin from a recent congregational Communion service to help the participants reflect upon the specifics of how the sacrament is administered in your congregation. Ask the questions "Why do we do this?" and "How does this relate to the baptismal covenant?" as you look at different parts of the service.

3. Review the section "Called to Ministry" beginning on page 44 and the section "Baptism and Christian Ministry" in *By Water and the Spirit*. *The Book of Discipline—2004* includes this thought-provoking statement about the ministry of daily life to which laypeople are commissioned in their baptism: "The people of God, who are the church made visible in the world, must convince the world of the reality of the gospel or leave it unconvinced. There can be no evasion or delegation of this responsibility; the church is either faithful as a witnessing and serving community, or it loses its vitality and its impact on an unbelieving world" (¶ 128). Ask the participants to consider the differences that might occur in their family, congregation, and community if all Christians lived out the ministry they are called to through baptism. Invite the participants to reflect silently on how they understand their call to ministry. Allow willing participants to share any of their feelings or ideas.

4. Review the section "Marriage" beginning on page 45 and the section "Baptism and Christian Marriage" in *By Water and the Spirit*. Have the group read the "A Service of Christian Marriage," which begins on page 864 in the *Hymnal*. Call attention to the frequent references to a covenant, as well as to baptism. Look closely at the "Dismissal with Blessing" (p. 869). These beautiful words show that marriage is closely related to ministry for Christians. Encourage the group to examine this relationship.

5. Review the section "Death and Resurrection" beginning on page 46 and the section "Baptism and Christian Funeral" in *By Water and the Spirit*. Have the group read the "Service of Death and Resurrection," which begins on page 870 in the *Hymnal*. Talk about what this service says about Christian living as well as Christian dying.

6. Review the section "So What?" beginning on page 47 and the section "Conclusion" in *By Water and the Spirit*. Let the participants identify important things they have learned and insights they have had during this study. As a group identify areas within the life of the congregation that need to be reexamined in light of the baptismal covenant. Encourage the participants to think about the most helpful way to begin the process of reexamination. Remind the participants that, although this is the last session of this study, living into our baptism is a lifelong endeavor.

7. Close the session with a service of Reaffirmation of the Baptismal Covenant. See page 50 of the *Hymnal* for an order of worship.

TO EXPAND THIS STUDY
- The call to discipleship and ministry is one that goes against many values and practices of the secular world. Read and discuss this quotation from *Christian Spiritual Formation in the Church and Classroom* by Susanne Johnson:

  > Inasmuch as it incorporates us into a community living under the commandment to radical equality, hospitality, and inclusiveness, baptism is the foe of any form of exclusion from the church's worship, witness, and work. Baptism is the sacrament of radical equality. The strongest statements of equality in the New Testament occur in the context of baptismal liturgy (Galatians 3:27-28).

In baptismal waters, all human distinctions that keep us unequal are washed away! Baptism proclaims freedom, mutuality, and shared leadership. Through baptism we each are ordained into the priesthood of all believers, disallowing any clerical or gender bias to the ministry of the church....If the baptismal liturgy is true, then many problems related to justice owe to our failure to appropriate the gifts and demands of our baptism (pp. 84-85).

- John and Charles Wesley published more than one hundred hymns on the Lord's Supper. One of the best is "O the Depth of Love Divine" (No. 627 in the *Hymnal*). Read aloud this great hymn, which marvels at the mystery of God's grace in the sacrament.

- Additional helpful material for your study of Christian marriage can be found in *The Book of Worship* beginning on page 115. Notice the service for "The Reaffirmation of the Marriage Covenant" on pages 135-38. Helpful material for your study of Christian death and resurrection can be found beginning on page 139.

- Many congregations have wedding policies that guide procedures. If your church has these types of policies, review them in light of the material presented in this session. The following questions may be helpful:
Do our policies help prepare couples for a Christian marriage?
Do our policies help all participants understand that the wedding is a service of Christian worship?
Do our policies help couples understand the relationship between their baptism and marriage covenant?

- Study the relationships between baptism, death, life, and resurrection as Paul presents them in Romans 6:3-11.

- If there are people in the study who are inquiring about ordained ministry or some other form of commissioned (or certified) ministry, assist them in securing a copy of *The Christian as Minister*. (Available from Cokesbury.)

Historical Divisions in the Christian Church

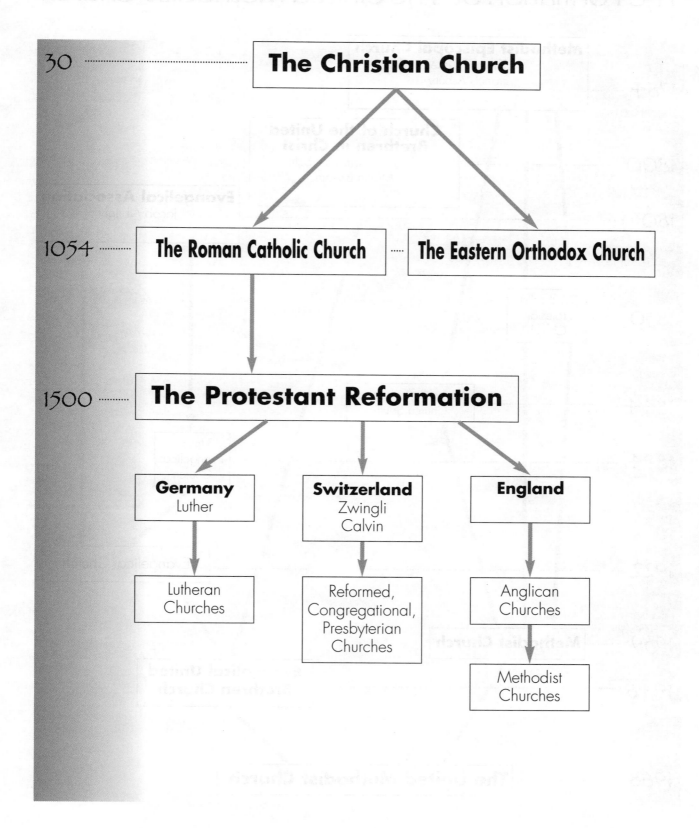

30	**The Christian Church**
1054	**The Roman Catholic Church** **The Eastern Orthodox Church**
1500	**The Protestant Reformation**

Germany
Luther

Switzerland
Zwingli
Calvin

England

Lutheran
Churches

Reformed,
Congregational,
Presbyterian
Churches

Anglican
Churches

Methodist
Churches

The Formation of The United Methodist Church

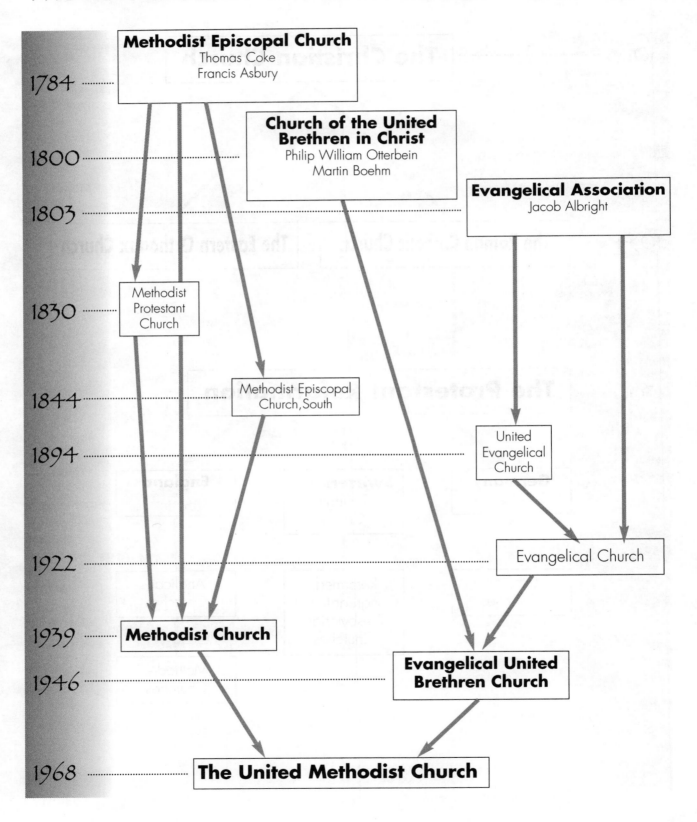

1784	**Methodist Episcopal Church** — Thomas Coke, Francis Asbury
1800	**Church of the United Brethren in Christ** — Philip William Otterbein, Martin Boehm
1803	**Evangelical Association** — Jacob Albright
1830	Methodist Protestant Church
1844	Methodist Episcopal Church, South
1894	United Evangelical Church
1922	Evangelical Church
1939	**Methodist Church**
1946	**Evangelical United Brethren Church**
1968	**The United Methodist Church**

APPENDIX—
THE Baptismal Covenant I

HOLY BAPTISM
CONFIRMATION
REAFFIRMATION OF FAITH
RECEPTION INTO THE
UNITED METHODIST CHURCH
RECEPTION INTO A LOCAL CONGREGATION

This service may be used for any of the above acts, or any combination of these that may be called for on a given occasion.

INTRODUCTION TO THE SERVICE

As persons are coming forward, an appropriate hymn of baptism or confirmation may be sung.

1 *The pastor makes the following statement to the congregation:*

Brothers and sisters in Christ:
Through the Sacrament of Baptism
    we are initiated into Christ's holy church.
We are incorporated into God's mighty acts
        of salvation
    and given new birth through water and the Spirit.
All this is God's gift, offered to us without price.

2 *If there are confirmations or reaffirmations, the pastor continues:*

Through confirmation,
    and through the reaffirmation of our faith,
    we renew the covenant declared at our baptism,
    acknowledge what God is doing for us,
    and affirm our commitment to Christ's holy church.

PRESENTATION OF CANDIDATES

3 *A representative of the congregation presents the candidates with the appropriate statements:*

I present *Name(s)* for baptism.
I present *Name(s)* for confirmation.
I present *Name(s)* to affirm *their* faith.
I present *Name(s)* who come(s) to this congregation
from the _____ Church.

RENUNCIATION OF SIN AND PROFESSION OF FAITH

4 *The pastor addresses parents or other sponsors and those candidates who can answer for themselves:*

On behalf of the whole church, I ask you:
Do you renounce the spiritual forces of wickedness,
    reject the evil powers of this world,
    and repent of your sin?

I do.

Do you accept the freedom and power God gives you
    to resist evil, injustice, and oppression
    in whatever forms they present themselves?

I do.

Do you confess Jesus Christ as your Savior,
put your whole trust in his grace,
and promise to serve him as your Lord,
in union with the church which Christ has opened
    to people of all ages, nations, and races?

I do.

5 *The pastor addresses parents or other sponsors of candidates not able to answer for themselves:*

Will you nurture *these children (persons)*
in Christ's holy church,
that by your teaching and example *they* may be guided
    to accept God's grace for *themselves,*
    to profess *their* faith openly,
    and to lead a Christian life?

I will.

6 *The pastor addresses candidates who can answer for themselves:*

According to the grace given to you,
will you remain *faithful members* of Christ's holy church
and serve as Christ's *representatives* in the world?

I will.

7 *If those who have answered for themselves have sponsors, the pastor addresses the sponsors:*

Will you who sponsor *these candidates* support and encourage *them* in *their* Christian life?

I will.

8 *The pastor addresses the congregation:*

Do you, as Christ's body, the church, reaffirm both your rejection of sin and your commitment to Christ?

We do.

Will you nurture one another in the Christian faith and life and include *these persons* now before you in your care?

With God's help we will proclaim the good news and live according to the example of Christ. We will surround *these persons* with a community of love and forgiveness, that *they* may grow in *their* trust of God, and be found faithful in *their* service to others. We will pray for *them*, that *they* may be true disciples who walk in the way that leads to life.

9 *The pastor addresses all:*

Let us join together in professing the Christian faith as contained in the Scriptures of the Old and New Testaments.

Do you believe in God the Father?

I believe in God, the Father Almighty, creator of heaven and earth.

Do you believe in Jesus Christ?

I believe in Jesus Christ, his only Son, our Lord, [who was conceived by the Holy Spirit, born of the Virgin Mary, suffered under Pontius Pilate, was crucified, died, and was buried; he descended to the dead. On the third day he rose again; he ascended into heaven, is seated at the right hand of the Father, and will come again to judge the living and the dead.]

Do you believe in the Holy Spirit?

I believe in the Holy Spirit, [the holy catholic* church, the communion of saints, the forgiveness of sins, the resurrection of the body, and the life everlasting.]

* *universal*

THANKSGIVING OVER THE WATER

10 *If there are baptisms, or if water is to be used for reaffirmation, the water may be poured into the font at this time, and the following prayer offered:*

The Lord be with you.

And also with you.

Let us pray.

Eternal Father:
When nothing existed but chaos,
    you swept across the dark waters
    and brought forth light.
In the days of Noah
    you saved those on the ark through water.
After the flood you set in the clouds a rainbow.
When you saw your people as slaves in Egypt,
    you led them to freedom through the sea.
Their children you brought through the Jordan
    to the land which you promised.

**Sing to the Lord, all the earth.
Tell of God's mercy each day.**

In the fullness of time you sent Jesus,
    nurtured in the water of a womb.
He was baptized by John and anointed by your Spirit.
He called his disciples
    to share in the baptism of his death
        and resurrection
    and to make disciples of all nations.

**Declare his works to the nations,
his glory among all the people.**

Pour out your Holy Spirit,
to bless this gift of water and *those* who *receive* it,
to wash away *their* sin

and clothe *them* in righteousness
    throughout *their lives*,
that, dying and being raised with Christ,
    they may share in his final victory.

**All praise to you, Eternal Father,
through your Son Jesus Christ,
who with you and the Holy Spirit
lives and reigns for ever.
Amen.**

BAPTISM WITH LAYING ON OF HANDS

11 *As each candidate is baptized, the pastor says:*

Name, I baptize you in the name of the Father,
    and of the Son, and of the Holy Spirit.

The people respond:

Amen.

*Immediately after the administration of the water,
the pastor, and others if desired, place hands on the
head of each candidate, as the pastor says to each:*

The Holy Spirit work within you,
that being born through water and the Spirit,
you may be a faithful disciple of Jesus Christ.

The people respond:

Amen.

*When all candidates have been baptized, the pas-
tor invites the congregation to welcome them:*

Now it is our joy to welcome our new *sisters and
brothers* in Christ.

**Through baptism
you are incorporated by the Holy Spirit
    into God's new creation
and made to share in Christ's royal priesthood.
We are all one in Christ Jesus.
With joy and thanksgiving we welcome you
    as *members* of the family of Christ.**

CONFIRMATION OR REAFFIRMATION OF FAITH

12 *Here water may be used symbolically in ways
    that cannot be interpreted as baptism, as the
    pastor says:*

Remember your baptism and be thankful.

Amen.

*As the pastor, and others if desired, place hands on
the head of each person being confirmed or reaffirming faith, the pastor says to each:*

Name, the Holy Spirit work within you,
that having been born through water and the Spirit,
you may live as a faithful disciple of Jesus Christ.

All respond:

Amen.

13 *When there is a congregational reaffirmation of
    the Baptismal Covenant, water may be used
    symbolically in ways that cannot be interpreted
    as baptism, as the pastor says:*

Remember your baptism and be thankful.

Amen.

RECEPTION INTO
THE UNITED METHODIST CHURCH

14 *If there are persons coming into membership in
    The United Methodist Church from other
    denominations who have not yet been presented,
    they may be presented at this time.*

*The pastor addresses all those transferring their mem-
bership into The United Methodist Church, together
with those who, through baptism or in confirmation,
have just professed their own faith:*

As *members* of Christ's universal church,
will you be loyal to The United Methodist Church,
and do all in your power to strengthen its ministries?

I will.

RECEPTION INTO THE LOCAL CONGREGATION

15 *If there are persons joining this congregation
    from other United Methodist congregations who
    have not yet been presented, they may be pre-
    sented at this time.*

*The pastor addresses all those transferring mem-
bership into the congregation and those who have
just professed their own faith, in baptism or in
confirmation:*

As *members* of this congregation,
will you faithfully participate in its ministries
    by your prayers, your presence,
    your gifts, and your service?

I will.

COMMENDATION AND WELCOME

16 *The pastor addresses the congregation:*

Members of the household of God,
I commend *these persons* to your love and care.
Do all in your power to increase *their* faith,
    confirm *their* hope, and perfect *them* in love.

The congregation responds:

**We give thanks for all that God
    has already given you
  and we welcome you in Christian love.
As members together with you
    in the body of Christ
    and in this congregation
    of The United Methodist Church,
we renew our covenant
    faithfully to participate
    in the ministries of the church
    by our prayers, our presence,
    our gifts, and our service,
that in everything God may be glorified
    through Jesus Christ.**

The pastor addresses those baptized, confirmed, or received:

The God of all grace,
    who has called us to eternal glory in Christ,
establish you and strengthen you
    by the power of the Holy Spirit,
that you may live in grace and peace.

One or more lay leaders may join with the pastor in acts of welcome and peace.

Appropriate thanksgivings and intercessions for those who have participated in these acts should be included in the concerns and prayers which follow.

It is most fitting that the service continue with Holy Communion, in which the union of the new members with the body of Christ is most fully expressed. The new members may receive first.

Disciplinary Items

ARTICLE XVII—OF BAPTISM

Baptism is not only a sign of profession and mark of difference whereby Christians are distinguished from others that are not baptized; but it is also a sign of regeneration or the new birth. The Baptism of young children is to be retained in the Church.

(From "The Articles of Religion of The Methodist Church," p. 63, *The Book of Discipline—2004.*)

ARTICLE VI—THE SACRAMENTS

We believe the Sacraments, ordained by Christ, are symbols and pledges of the Christian's profession and of God's love toward us. They are means of grace by which God works invisibly in us, quickening, strengthening and confirming our faith in him. Two Sacraments are ordained by Christ our Lord, namely Baptism and the Lord's Supper.

We believe Baptism signifies entrance into the household of faith, and is a symbol of repentance and inner cleansing from sin, a representation of the new birth in Christ Jesus and a mark of Christian discipleship.

We believe children are under the atonement of Christ and as heirs of the Kingdom of God are acceptable subjects for Christian Baptism. Children of believing parents through Baptism become the special responsibility of the Church. They should be nurtured and led to personal acceptance of Christ, and by profession of faith confirm their Baptism.

We believe the Lord's Supper is a representation of our redemption, a memorial of the sufferings and death of Christ, and a token of love and union which Christians have with Christ and with one another. Those who rightly, worthily and in faith eat the broken bread and drink the blessed cup partake of the body and blood of Christ in a spiritual manner until he comes.

(From "The Confession of Faith of the Evangelical United Brethren Church," p. 68, *The Book of Discipline—2004.*)

¶ **218.** *Growth in Faithful Discipleship*—Faithful membership in the local church is essential for personal growth and for developing a deeper commitment to the will and grace of God. As members involve themselves in private and public prayer, worship, the sacraments, study, Christian action, systematic giving, and holy discipline, they grow in their appreciation of Christ, understanding of God at work in history and the natural order, and an understanding of themselves.

¶ **219.** *Mutual Responsibility*—Faithful discipleship includes the obligation to participate in the corporate life of the congregation with fellow members of the body of Christ. A member is bound in sacred covenant to shoulder the burdens, share the risks, and celebrate the joys of fellow members. A Christian is called to speak the truth in love, always ready to confront conflict in the spirit of forgiveness and reconciliation.

APPENDIX—
Helpful Resources

Baptism: Christ's Act in the Church, by Laurence Hull Stookey (Abingdon, 1982).

Baptism, Eucharist and Ministry (World Council of Churches, 1982).

El Bautismo: Puerta de Entrada a Una Nueva Vida en Cristo, by Aquiles Ernesto Martínez (Discipleship Resources, 2004).

Christian Spiritual Formation in the Church and Classroom, by Susanne Johnson (Abingdon, 1989).

Come to the Waters: Baptism and Our Ministry of Welcoming Seekers and Making Disciples, by Daniel Benedict (Discipleship Resources, 1997).

Documents of the Baptismal Liturgy, by E. C. Whitaker, revised and expanded by Maxwell E. Johnson (Liturgical Press, 2003).

Holy People: A Liturgical Ecclesiology, by Gordon W. Lathrop (Augsburg Fortress, 1999).

A Place for Baptism, by Regina Kuehn (Liturgy Training Publications, 1992).

Remember Who You Are: Baptism, a Model for Christian Life, by William H. Willimon (The Upper Room, Rev. Ed. 1999).

Sacraments and Discipleship, by Mark W. Stamm (Discipleship Resources, 2000).

Sacraments as God's Self Giving: Understanding Baptism and the Lords Supper in a United Methodist Context, by James F. White (Abingdon, Rev. Ed. 2001).

This Gift of Water: The Practice and Theology of Baptism Among Methodists in America, by Gayle Carlton Felton (Abingdon, 1993).

Worship Matters Volume 2: A United Methodist Guide to Worship Work, by E. Byron Anderson (Discipleship Resources, 1999).

Resources published by Discipleship Resources may be ordered by phone at 800-972-0433, online at www.upperroom.org/bookstore, or from Christian bookstores.